100

WAYNE THIEBAUD **100**

Paintings, Prints, and Drawings

WAYNE THIEBAUD **100**
Paintings, Prints, and Drawings

Scott A. Shields, PhD

with essays by
Margaretta Markle Lovell, PhD
Hearne Pardee
Julia Friedman, PhD

chronology by
Mary Okin

PORTLAND, OREGON

Pomegranate Communications, Inc.
19018 NE Portal Way, Portland, OR 97230
800-227-1428   pomegranate.com

To learn about new releases and special offers from Pomegranate, please visit pomegranate.com and sign up for our newsletter. For all other queries, see "Contact Us" on our home page.

Published on the occasion of the exhibition *Wayne Thiebaud 100: Paintings, Prints, and Drawings*
Crocker Art Museum, Sacramento, California: October 11, 2020–January 3, 2021
Toledo Museum of Art, Toledo, Ohio: February 6–May 2, 2021
Dixon Gallery and Gardens, Memphis, Tennessee: July 25–October 3, 2021
McNay Art Museum, San Antonio, Texas: October 28, 2021–January 16, 2022
Brandywine Conservancy & Museum of Art, Chadds Ford, Pennsylvania: February 5–May 8, 2022

COVER: *Pies, Pies, Pies*, 1961. Oil on canvas, 20 x 30 in. Crocker Art Museum, gift of Philip L. Ehlert in memory of Dorothy Evelyn Ehlert, 1974.12

FRONTISPIECE: *Wayne Thiebaud in his Sacramento studio*, 1987. Photograph by Matt Bult

Library of Congress Cataloging-in-Publication Data

Names: Shields, Scott A. | Lovell, Margaretta Markle, 1944- | Pardee,
   Hearne. | Friedman, Julia P. | Okin, Mary. | Crocker Art Museum,
   organizer, host institution. | Toledo Museum of Art, host institution. |
   Dixon Gallery and Gardens, host institution. | McNay Art Museum, host
   institution. | Brandywine Conservancy & Museum of Art, host institution.

Title: Wayne Thiebaud 100 : paintings, prints, and drawings / Scott A.
   Shields, PhD ; with essays by Margaretta Markle Lovell, PhD, Hearne
   Pardee, Julia Friedman, PhD ; chronology by Mary Okin.
Other titles: Wayne Thiebaud one hundred
Description: Portland, Oregon : Pomegranate, 2020. | Includes
   bibliographical references and index.
Identifiers: LCCN 2020007756 | ISBN 9781087501178 (hardcover)
Subjects: LCSH: Thiebaud, Wayne--Exhibitions.
Classification: LCC N6537.T4735 A4 2020 | DDC 759.13--dc23
LC record available at https://lccn.loc.gov/2020001422

Pomegranate Item No. A295
Designed by Stephanie Odeh
Printed in China

29 28 27 26 25 24 23 22 21 20   10 9 8 7 6 5 4 3 2 1

CONTENTS

PREFACE AND ACKNOWLEDGMENTS

That the sensual life if ordered densely enough and treated intelligently enough could be art, that dessert was a large enough subject for an artist if the artist were willing to give it the same intensity of purpose that had once been reserved for religion, that the things of this world were enough if you cared about them enough— all of these lessons could be learned from Wayne Thiebaud's pictures, and were.

—Adam Gopnik, "An American Painter" (2000)[1]

To celebrate the 100th birthday of Sacramento's most renowned artist, the Crocker Art Museum presents *Wayne Thiebaud 100: Paintings, Prints, and Drawings.* Best known for his tantalizing paintings of desserts, Thiebaud has long been affiliated with Pop Art, though his body of work is far more expansive. This exhibition represents the artist's achievements in all media, with pieces drawn from the Crocker's holdings and the collections of the Thiebaud Family and Foundation—many of which, until now, have not been shown publicly. For the Crocker, the show continues a tradition of hosting a Thiebaud exhibition every decade since 1951, when the museum held the artist's first one-person show, *Influences on a Young Painter—Wayne Thiebaud*, an exhibition that, like the current exhibition, included work in all media.

Thiebaud's art has long been beloved in Sacramento, and today this is the case among audiences internationally. His presence has also had a great effect on Sacramento, impacting its sense of self and civic pride, as well as inspiring numerous artist- and non-artist-residents. Sacramento has likewise had a great influence on Thiebaud, who is quick to acknowledge the importance of making art connoting shared experiences. Sacramentans, obviously, have experienced many of the same things that Thiebaud has, because the artist derives so much of his subject matter locally. As Thiebaud himself has said, "To be local is the touchstone of what you are and where you come from, what you're seeing."[2] Sacramento's shop windows, state fair, neighborhood bakeries and delis, citizenry, and river landscapes have all factored into his paintings.

And, as in the Crocker's eight solo Thiebaud exhibitions of decades past, the community has very much been a part of this effort. We are especially grateful to title sponsor Marcy Friedman; presenting sponsor Hughey Phillips, LLP; signature sponsor Joyce and Jim Teel; and exhibition sponsors Ted and Melza Barr; Steven and Pam Eggert; Sylvia Fitzgerald, ISA AM; Melinda and Clement Kong; Linda M. Lawrence; Mary Lou Stone; Julie and Michael Teel; and Pamela Heid Zaiss and Conrad Zaiss. Additional catalogue sponsors graciously helped underwrite this publication. They include Barbara Arnold and Henry Go; Lynne Cannady and David Ford; Simon K. Chiu; Susan K. Edling; Joan

Wayne Thiebaud demonstrating painting at Rice University in Houston, Texas, 1971. Photographer unknown

and Richard F. Gann; Will H. Green, MD, and Martin Palomar; Dr. Kathleen J. Greene; Raymond Gundlach and Laurie Wood-Gundlach; Patricia and Donald Ingoglia Family; Dorothy and Norm Lien; Margaux and Robert McMillan; Janet Mohle-Boetani, MD; Paul and Susan Prudler; Simone Miller Rathe and Mark Rathe; David and Patricia Schwartz; Kimi Sue Swaback in honor of Käthe Swaback; David Townsend and Sharon Usher; and Frank and Helen Wheeler. Numerous others made important contributions to this endeavor as well.

Throughout the process, Colleen Casey, director of LeBaron's Fine Art, has been instrumental, helping to assemble the checklist and catalogue, answer questions, oversee photo shoots, and serve as the liaison to Wayne. Thiebaud's son and daughter-in-law, Matt and Maria Bult, have also been enormously helpful, providing information, images, and loans from their collection and from the Wayne Thiebaud Foundation.

An excellent team of authors has come together to write the catalogue text. In addition to an introduction and first chapter by Scott A. Shields, essays by Margaretta Markle Lovell, Hearne Pardee, and Julia Friedman have each contributed to our understanding of Thiebaud's achievements in specific genres and media. Mary Okin compiled a 100-year chronology of the artist's life; LeBaron's Fine Art provided the bibliography.

Four museums across the United States will host the exhibition after its Crocker debut: the Toledo Museum of Art in Ohio; the Dixon Gallery and Gardens in Memphis, Tennessee; the McNay Art Museum in San Antonio, Texas; and the Brandywine Conservancy & Museum of Art in Chadds Ford, Pennsylvania. We appreciate each of these institutions and their directors for supporting the show and the work.

In Sacramento, we acknowledge the Crocker Art Museum's co-trustees and staff. We especially recognize Christie Hajela, who oversaw the project's many moving parts, not only at the Crocker but also at other venues,

just as Mariah Briel procured images and assisted with catalogue editing and documentation. Erin Aitali coordinated loans, photography, and shipping arrangements; Matthew Isble oversaw the Crocker's installation; and Cristina Urrutia assisted from start to finish. Many of the photographs in the catalogue were taken by Gerard Vuilleumier with the help of Simon K. Chiu, the high quality of their images making this volume more beautiful.

For creating such an important publication, we thank Zoe Katherine Burke, publisher of Pomegranate Communications, Inc., whose team includes Alyssa Flynn, copywriter; Jennifer Messinger, production coordinator; Linda Meyer, editor; Cory Mimms, publishing manager; Patrice Morris, art director; and Stephanie Odeh, senior designer.

Most of all, we acknowledge Wayne Thiebaud, who not only consented to the idea of another Crocker exhibition but also helped realize the show through meetings, interviews, loans of artwork, and ever-patient oversight. We thank him too for helping make the Sacramento region an art center of international importance and, especially, for creating a body of work that realizes the universal possibilities of things found close to home. ▲▼▲

Lial A. Jones
Mort and Marcy Friedman Director and CEO
Crocker Art Museum

Scott A. Shields
Associate Director and Chief Curator
Crocker Art Museum

NOTES

1   Adam Gopnik, "An American Painter," in Steven A. Nash and Adam Gopnik, *Wayne Thiebaud: A Paintings Retrospective* (San Francisco: Fine Arts Museums of San Francisco, 2000), 61.

2   Wayne Thiebaud, quoted in Elaine O'Brien, "Locating Thiebaud," in *Wayne Thiebaud: Works from 1955 to 2003* (Sacramento, CA: University Library Gallery, California State University, Sacramento, 2003), 61.

INTRODUCTION

This Is Not a Pie: Wayne Thiebaud and the Treachery of Images

Scott A. Shields

Based in observation and convincingly executed, Wayne Thiebaud's art looks real and often feels comfortingly familiar, qualities that have led most viewers to describe it as realist. At the same time, extended looking acknowledges the works' artifice, as Thiebaud filters it through his memory, knowledge of art history, and imagination, making it possible, as he states, "for representational painting to be both abstract and real simultaneously."[1] Only in his sketches and, to a certain degree, his representations of the human form, does Thiebaud directly record what's at hand. Most of his finished works are manipulations of reality, capturing what he knows or feels about an object or place, not just its appearance, a fusion he describes as being of three different worlds:

> There is (1) our real world, which we all share, and on which there is a consensus; (2) the art world, and its historical tradition; and (3) one's apperceptive mass, a unique individual world. These influences have to be of almost equal percentage in order to ensure a full visual experience.[2]

Though such a view seems perfectly logical today, it was, when Thiebaud was starting out, an abrupt departure from ideals held by the artistic avant-garde: the Abstract Expressionists. Clyfford Still, one of the most dogmatic and influential of these artists, is remembered to have stated, "I don't believe in historicity. I don't believe in museums. I don't believe in memory. I don't believe in the Renaissance."[3] Certainly this has never been the case for Thiebaud.

Nearly everything Thiebaud depicts is either man-made, mass-produced, or somehow processed. In terms of his still lifes, for which he is most famous, food is rarely straight from the garden (or orchard) but is manipulated and often laid out cafeteria-style, in orderly rows and display cases. He also often showcases a single type of food, such as pie or cake, a departure from the random assemblies of disparate objects so often depicted in the still lifes of art-historical tradition. "I'm interested in foods generally which have been fooled with ritualistically," he explains, "displays contrived and arranged in certain ways to tempt us or to seduce us or to religiously transcend us. There's something I find fascinating about making a circle of butter, hollowing a cantaloupe."[4]

Thiebaud's landscapes also evince human manipulation, which he then transforms even further. This is certainly the case with his city scenes, which he conceives though an assembly of sketches, an approach like that used by American artist Edward Hopper in his urban views. Even in Thiebaud's less trammeled landscapes, where human intervention is not so apparent, the implied presence of people remains critical to the work. "If that implication isn't there," he explains, "there's something uninhabitable about the picture."[5] This human-centered combination of reality and artifice is an integral part of what makes a Thiebaud a Thiebaud.

Boston Cremes (detail, pl. 9), 1962

The same is true of Thiebaud's paintings of people, though the figures, at least, are generally closer to their original source, as he most often works from models. He portrays people as having been shaped by time and place: their hairstyles and clothing are emblematic of their era; their faces suggest a familiar weariness associated with modern life; and their poses often connote isolation, even in groups. Even Thiebaud's animals, which he portrays infrequently, evidence contemporary life. A bird on a swing is an impossibly cute, domesticated, twentieth-century oddity, one that would be ill-equipped to survive in nature. His self-satisfied rabbit or, more accurately, bunny, has been bred for the Easter market—a distant, domestic descendant of Albrecht Dürer's wild and sinewy *Young Hare* of 1502 (figs. 1, 2).

Thiebaud makes subjects his own through his iconographic and compositional choices, paint application, distinctive light and palette, overt manipulation of perspective and scale, and by what he includes or omits. The placement of objects or people is of paramount expressive importance, as are barren settings expunged of extraneous detail, which help to bestow his subjects with their central focus and consequence. The harsh scrutiny of manufactured, fluorescent light is also emblematic of his work, as are his rainbow halations, which enliven the edges of his subjects and transition them into their stark backgrounds.

Thiebaud's concern with paint application and surface manifests his interest in the Abstract Expressionists—and earlier artistic movements and artists—though his goals are different. In Thiebaud's paintings, linear ridges of pigment help animate empty expanses and "'lock in' the planes and make them 'flatter,'" at the same time creating tension with the robust, shadowed three-dimensionality of his subjects.[6] Desserts are painted with luscious passages of pigment juxtaposed against those that are purely flat; dizzyingly steep San Francisco streets are a combination of shallow and deeply recessed space; Sacramento-San Joaquin Delta views combine scales and perspectives impossible in the real world. To manipulate reality so effectively, Thiebaud draws upon years of cartooning and illustrating, as well as decades of artmaking. Numerous semesters teaching art history have also played a role, providing the artist with a wealth of knowledge and source material to draw upon, including Western traditions such as trompe-l'oeil painting, Impressionism, Fauvism, Abstract Expressionism, and Bay Area Figuration, as well as arts of the Middle East, China, and India. Cartoons and illustrations by other artists have factored in as well.

Surrealism also contributes significantly to Thiebaud's practice, though it has been less frequently acknowledged. Artist Barnett Newman made this connection early on, stating, "Those European surrealists are boys compared to what you can do with a gumball machine. That's a real surreal object in you."[7] More recently, art historian Pepe Karmel has called Thiebaud's art "metaphysical," noting its relationship to works by Italian masters, including Carlo Carrà, Giorgio de Chirico, and Giorgio Morandi, as well as Americans like Georgia O'Keeffe, Charles Sheeler, and Edward Hopper. "Like them," Karmel explains, "he [Thiebaud] makes the everyday world seem suddenly unfamiliar, the most commonplace object charged with unspeakable significance."[8] Thiebaud himself concedes the Surrealist connection as "legitimate."[9]

Thiebaud does not practice the automatist aspects of Surrealism, however, as his work is not spontaneously achieved but rather deliberate, with plenty of time for decision-making, even though he improvises as he goes. He often starts with his own thumbnail sketches, which he calls "thinking drawings"—also "scientific research papers"—an approach far removed from Surrealist automatism (or, later, Abstract Expressionist improvisation).[10]

For Thiebaud, drawing is a way to "to test what one can know" about things, though relatively few of his drawings result in finished works.[11] When they do, these "little proposed paintings" are not generally translated in their entirety but sometimes used in part or in combination, the latter especially true of his city scenes.[12]

Although not automatist, Thiebaud's work is very much aligned with work by Surrealist and Metaphysical painters who sought to make familiar objects emotive or strange—or, as Thiebaud describes, "other-worldly."[13] In fact, the kind of representational painting that he admires most comes from painters who combine "perceptual manifestations and conceptual enterprises"—painters like de Chirico and Morandi.[14] De Chirico, who Thiebaud describes as a "big influence," sought to arrest the sensations that familiar things could evoke. He also exploited multiple vanishing points that informed Thiebaud's own manipulation of urban San Francisco and the rural Sacramento-San Joaquin Delta.[15] Thiebaud has called de Chirico "one of the most indelible kind of painters . . . like a tattoo," suggesting the lingering effect the work could have on one's psyche.[16]

Aesthetically, however, Thiebaud's paintings bear little resemblance to de Chirico's, though they do have striking similarities to the enigmatically unassuming still lifes of Morandi. Thiebaud's still-life subjects are bolder than Morandi's and frequently accorded more importance than they perhaps deserve. The objects in Morandi's paintings are clustered, subtle, and sometimes unrecognizable, which makes them less significant in and of themselves (fig. 3). Thiebaud instead chooses his subjects for their broad familiarity and communicative potential. Because he does not render them from life but from memory and imagination, they are reduced to their essentials. "I made it a point to paint the pies, the gumball machines, the cakes, etc., as I remembered them. And this is perhaps

Fig. 1. **Rabbit**, 1971. Lithograph, three colors on Arches paper, number 37/50, 22¼ x 30 in. Acquavella Galleries, New York

Fig. 2. Albrecht Dürer (German, 1471–1528), **Young Hare**, 1502. Watercolor, 9⅞ x 8⅞ in. The Albertina Museum, Vienna

|11|

what makes them seem like icons, in a sense. They're greatly conventionalized."[17]

A compelling progenitor for Thiebaud's practice of inflating the importance of everyday things is the Belgian Surrealist René Magritte, whose iconic placement of everyday objects against spare backgrounds—apples, rocks, candles, bowlers, and, most famously, a pipe—

Fig. 3. Giorgio Morandi (Italian, 1890–1964), *Still Life with a Bottle*, c. 1951. Oil on canvas, 17 x 18½ in. Toledo Museum of Art, Toledo, Ohio, purchased with funds from the Libby Endowment, gift of Edward Drummond Libbey, 1952.142

provide compelling prototypes for Thiebaud's depictions of hats, cigars, and pairs of shoes. Both Magritte and Thiebaud had beginnings in the commercial realm, which certainly informed their similar approaches to subject matter and composition, even down to the way each rendered multiple tiny compositions on a single sheet, like a storyboard, to test out ideas and determine which worked best.[18] There is also a subtle, tongue-in-cheek humor that underlies both artists' work.

Magritte's focus on the dialectics between an object's realism and the artificiality of its representation has also been one of Thiebaud's enduring interests. Magritte's 1929 *The Treachery of Images*, his well-known painting of an ordinary pipe accompanied by the inscription *"Ceci n'est pas une pipe"* ("This is not a pipe"), is a compositional and conceptual precursor to Thiebaud's still lifes of common foods and objects (fig. 4). French historian and philosopher Michel Foucault referred to Magritte's work as a "simple notion or fantasy of a pipe," a description equally apt for Thiebaud's still-life subjects.[19] Like Magritte's pipe, Thiebaud's pies, cakes, hot dogs, and gumball machines are simple notions or codifications of an object's semblance in the mind's eye, as opposed to a veritable representation of actual appearance. Thiebaud explains:

> A problem that I think is a continuing one is attempting to distinguish between objective, perceptual information and the attempt to distill or codify or symbolically refer to it, as opposed to memory, fantasy, and a lot of other kinds of references. Our minds are filled with conventions, which means convenient ways of doing something, or a cliché, which is probably the same thing. . . . When you look at an object in comparison with these conventions, you're faced with a real dilemma, one which I propose is unending, because you can never see everything that's there.[20]

As portrayed, Thiebaud's objects are an intensification of that which is most memorable: an essence caught and set down, a distillation of reality rather than realty itself. Thiebaud appropriately likens this process to cooking, stating, "When you reduce a sauce, you do so in order to improve it by taking out those

Fig. 4. René Magritte (Belgian, 1898–1967), *The Treachery of Images (This Is Not a Pipe)*, 1929. Oil on canvas, 23¾ x 31¹⁵⁄₁₆ x 1 in. Los Angeles County Museum of Art, purchased with funds provided by the Mr. and Mrs. William Preston Harrison Collection, 78.7. Photograph © 2019 Museum Associates / LACMA. Licensed by Art Resource, NY

ingredients you no longer need. The same is true of realist painting: you reduce it by essentialization."[21] Foucault describes Magritte's iconic pipe in a similar (though less colloquial) way:

> Without saying anything, a mute and adequately recognizable figure displays the object in its essence. . . . Now, compared to the traditional function of the legend, Magritte's text is doubly paradoxical. It sets out to name something that evidently does not need to be named (the form is too well known, the label too familiar). And at the moment when he should reveal the name, Magritte does so by denying that the object is what it is.[22]

Foucault called Magritte's painting a "calligram," a union of text and imagery that Magritte then proceeded to unravel. The philosopher explained, "The calligram aspires playfully to efface the oldest oppositions of our alphabetical civilization: to show and to name; to shape and to say; to reproduce and to articulate; to imitate and to signify; to look at and to read."[23] Thiebaud's paintings operate similarly in that the pigment, as he uses it, seeks to become its referent in a compelling combination of trompe-l'oeil illusionism and expressive brushwork. In 1964, art writer John Coplans described Thiebaud's still lifes as visual "puns," because the paint replicates the sticky surfaces and colors of mass-produced foods.[24] This was, as Thiebaud explained, a play on the truth that grew out of his exploration of materials: "While it is clearly in the line of 'trick-of-the-eye' painting where the artist is like a magician, I would like to show my hand and expose the trick, allowing the thrill of self-discovery and the ability to see oneself having the illusion."[25] As with Magritte's representation of a pipe, the illusions Thiebaud creates are not reality.

Thiebaud himself is quick to acknowledge the fiction of his art, and he has described art-making—drawing in particular—as an "unnatural act" because it asks the artist to "lie."[26] "Painting's great possibility is fiction, illusion," he states. "That's its magic, anyway. And if it's to continue, for me at least, it has to inquire after those aspects of the world in terms of transposition or interpretation or an extension."[27] Such ideas are critical to Thiebaud's art and are far different from those held by the Abstract Expressionists before him, who collectively promoted that a work of art as a physical object was reality enough—that it did not have to depict anything else to justify its existence. And yet, for Thiebaud, even if art was to be representational it needed to become a "fictionalized version of what's there," not a straightforward visual recording.[28]

Thiebaud does retain vestiges of Abstract Expressionism's "art-is-enough" ideals in his brushwork and in the underlying abstraction of his imagery, which enables his paintings to "work" on a formal level. But he, like his hero Willem de Kooning and the Bay Area Figurative painters of California (Richard Diebenkorn being the most important), came to determine that people, places, and things introduced meaning in a way that pure nonobjectivity could not. For these artists and others, the return to subject matter was more by necessity than choice, for by the middle of the 1950s the possibilities of painterly abstraction, at least according to Clement Greenberg, the era's preeminent art critic, had been "exhausted."[29]

At first, some artists reintroduced recognizable subject matter but with an Abstract Expressionist approach. Others then moved on to more clearly defined forms and imagery, the commonality and graphic nature of their production giving rise to the term Pop. In his own mature paintings, Thiebaud pursued a realism greater than that of de Kooning or of his Bay Area Figurative colleagues in California, and yet, the distance separating his work from theirs is perhaps not as great as the gap that separates his work from Pop, the label most often associated with Thiebaud's work.

To be sure, Thiebaud's paint application would be hard to imagine were it not for the Abstract Expressionists before him, though it is also traceable to earlier sources. Thiebaud's brushstrokes are not short, choppy swatches but carefully laid swaths, often of several inches or even feet, applied wet-on-wet with a *premier-coup* ("first strike") technique that Thiebaud admires in the work of Spanish master Diego Velázquez, the nineteenth-century Italian Macchiaioli painters, the American expatriate portraitist John Singer Sargent, and the Spanish Impressionist Joaquín Sorolla.[30] The pale and articulate facture of still lifes by Morandi also provided direction, as did, of course, the bolder, statement-making approach of de Kooning and the Bay Area Figuratives. Thiebaud's early experience as a commercial sign painter was also critical,

providing him with the technical training necessary to confidently lay down a stroke of paint.

Although Thiebaud's brushwork often calls attention to itself, it is also deliberate and precise, showcasing a restraint far removed from the Abstract Expressionists' improvisational, freewheeling approach. It nevertheless allows viewers to follow his path up, down, and sideways, filling forms and tracing the outlines of food, buildings, landscapes, and people in ways that best connote texture and mass. Sometimes brushwork subtly animates large, flat expanses—keeping these areas of "empty space" from becoming boring—the paint "combed" like the manicured sands of a Zen garden.[31] In other areas, pigment is built up with thick impasto that artfully details—and frequently mimics—his subjects.

The latter is most consistently true of Thiebaud's still lifes—especially pie, cake, and ice cream—in which paint can turn almost magically into what it seeks to depict or, as Foucault would say, "signs invok[ing] the very thing of which they speak."[32] This is so true of Thiebaud's depictions of food that one can literally become hungry looking at them. To emulate frosting, for instance, he "whips" his pigment until he can pretend he is actually icing the cake.[33] Though this approach is most conducive to desserts, there are numerous other examples throughout Thiebaud's oeuvre. Combed brushstrokes can suggest hair or fur; a squiggle of yellow or red can equal mustard or ketchup; shiny black swaths can become shoe polish; ridged pigment can echo earth strata or a rocky cliff; and a scumbled surface can connote dirty streets. Even today, in his most recent series of circus clowns, Thiebaud's earlier forays into depicting beauty products (or the application of makeup) has literally been put under a spotlight. Here, clown face paint becomes synonymous with its referent; the sign becomes the signifier.

Thiebaud has described this merging of form and content as "object transference."[34] Art historian Margaretta Lovell has called it "rhyming"—the "impasto 'rhymes' with the cake frosting, and the way [he's] making troughs in the paint rhymes with the way that a farmer tills his field."[35] Other Thiebaud writers have referred to the process as "simultaneity," Malcolm Warner, for instance, noting the artist's cleverness in selecting "willing subjects."[36] This is true not just of Thiebaud's paintings but of his work in other media as well. Thiebaud always asks himself whether oil, watercolor, pastel, or printmaking best lend themselves to particular subjects: "What sort of medium fits your image," he asks. "Is there a more legitimate medium for that?"[37]

Thiebaud's practice not only updates trompe-l'oeil tradition, it reinvestigates the concept of synesthesia, wherein one sense—in this case, sight—evokes another. Taste is most often at play here, but smell and touch also assume important roles. Sound is even suggested in some of his city and freeway subjects. Thiebaud also aims not to depict what something *looks* like as much as what it *feels* like. "I'm really a very strong sensualist," he says, "and that manifests itself in almost all the works."[38] And yet, passages of extraordinary realism are combined with sections blatantly false in flatness and simplification, creating tension and reminding viewers that this is, when all is said and done, just pigment on canvas. Areas of unabashed brushwork also expose the fraudulence of the scenes, the initial illusions crumbling as underlying abstraction and the painted surface take center stage.

In his well-known 1961 painting *Pies, Pies, Pies* (pl. 8), for example, Thiebaud emulates the fluffy meringues and creamy custards to whipped perfection. And yet, their colorful halation, flat unmodulated passages, and gravity-defying placement on a tilted tabletop—like Cézanne's

Fig. 5. Paul Cézanne (French, 1839–1906), **Still Life with Apples**, 1893–1894. Oil on canvas, 25¾ x 32⅛ in. J. Paul Getty Museum, Los Angeles, 96.PA.8

apples—acknowledge the artifice of the picture (fig. 5). Additionally, Thiebaud adds an extra dollop of thick paint, not on a piece of pie but on the table, and in the same color as the table itself, which brings its surface—and thus the picture plane—to the fore. There is no iconographic reason for this extra impasto swirl to be there; it is paint for paint's sake, and placed right above Thiebaud's signature, almost like a fingerprint. Something similar occurs in the artist's small *Cup of Coffee*, which he painted the same year (fig. 6). Here, most of the painterly activity is in the cream-colored background, the most obvious impasto flanking a horizontal swath at the bottom, which contains the artist's signature and date.

In some still lifes, including *Pie Slice* (1964; fig. 7), *Four Cupcakes* (1971), and *Three Treats* (c. 1972), Thiebaud places his signature directly below his subject almost as a compositional element, his stacking of imagery and text mirroring Magritte's pipe and its underlying written denial. Thiebaud, however, in typical fashion, fully grounds his three-dimensional objects with shadows, whereas Magritte allows his very sculptural pipe to float. But whereas Magritte's statement

|15|

Fig. 6. ***Cup of Coffee***, 1961. Oil on canvas, 18 x 12 in. The Fine Arts Collection, Jan Shrem and Maria Manetti Shrem Museum of Art, University of California, Davis, gift of Fay Nelson. Photograph by M. Lee Fatherree

denies the cliché and denounces the reality of his pipe, Thiebaud, by making his signature such a central part of the composition, seems to claim his desserts. Although he has been quoted as saying "It's not so much fun to be known as the pieman," in works like these at least, his signature seems to embrace his role as creator.[39]

Thiebaud lures his viewers into believing that what he presents is real, at least until extended looking reveals the hoax. He also denies his subjects too many specifics, allowing them to better conform to our collectively held ideal and transcend their actual importance. American writer and essayist Adam Gopnik, one of Thiebaud's most perceptive enthusiasts, calls the artist a literary painter, one capable of infusing even the smallest things with big meaning. "He has a writer's gift for making objects into symbols without betraying them as objects," Gopnik explains, "so that . . . a Thiebaud pie manages to suggest a world of longing—a serene abundance that is always a windowpane away—and yet remains a perfectly painted pie."[40] ▲▼▲

Fig. 7. **Pie Slice**, 1964. Oil on paperboard, 7½ x 8¾ in. Photograph courtesy of the Allan Stone Collection, New York

NOTES

1. Wayne Thiebaud, quoted in Mark Strand, ed., *Art of the Real: Nine American Figurative Painters* (New York: Clarkson N. Potter, 1983), 192.

2. Wayne Thiebaud, quoted in Richard Wollheim, "An Interview with Wayne Thiebaud," in *Wayne Thiebaud: Cityscapes* (San Francisco: Campbell-Thiebaud Gallery, 1993).

3. Dorr Bothwell quoting Clyfford Still, in Mary Fuller McChesney, *A Period of Exploration: San Francisco 1945–1950* (Oakland, CA: Oakland Museum Art Department, 1973), 36.

4. Wayne Thiebaud, quoted in Thomas Albright, "Wayne Thiebaud: Scrambling Around with Ordinary Problems," *Art News* 77, no. 2 (February 1978): 86.

5. Wayne Thiebaud, quoted in Bill Berkson, "Thiebaud on the Figure: An Interview by Bill Berkson" in *Wayne Thiebaud: Figurative Works 1959–1994* (South Bend, IN: Wiegand Gallery, College of Notre Dame, 1994).

6. Wayne Thiebaud, "Is a Lollipop Tree Worth Painting?" *San Francisco Sunday Chronicle*, July 15, 1962.

7. Barnett Newman, quoted by Wayne Thiebaud, oral history interview by Susan Larsen, May 17–18, 2001, transcript, Archives of American Art, Smithsonian Institution.

8. Pepe Karmel, "The Lonely Crowd: Men and Women in the Art of Wayne Thiebaud," in *Wayne Thiebaud*, by John Wilmerding (New York: Acquavella Galleries, 2012), 33–34.

9. Wayne Thiebaud, quoted in Eve Aschheim and Chris Daubert, *Episodes with Wayne Thiebaud: Four Interviews 2009–2011* (New York: Black Square Editions, 2014), 73.

10. Wayne Thiebaud, quoted in Constance W. Glenn, "Artist's Dialogue: A Conversation with Wayne Thiebaud," *Architectural Digest* 39, no. 9 (September 1982): 68; Wayne Thiebaud, quoted in Victoria Dalkey, *Wayne Thiebaud: Figure Drawings* (San Francisco: Campbell-Thiebaud Gallery, 1993), both cited in Isabelle Dervaux, *Wayne Thiebaud: Draftsman* (New York: Morgan Library and Museum, 2018), 115.

11. Wayne Thiebaud, quoted in Karen Tsujimoto, "Thiebaud: The Figure," in *Wayne Thiebaud: The Figure* (New York: Allan Stone Gallery, 2008), 6.

12. Thiebaud, quoted in Dervaux, *Draftsman*, 148.

13. Thiebaud, quoted in Aschheim and Daubert, *Episodes*, 73.

14. Steven A. Nash, "Unbalancing Acts: Wayne Thiebaud Reconsidered," in *Wayne Thiebaud: A Paintings Retrospective*, by Steven A. Nash and Adam Gopnik (San Francisco: Fine Arts Museums of San Francisco, 2000), 37n20; Meredith Tromble, "A Conversation with Wayne Thiebaud," *Artweek* 29 (January 1998): 15.

15. Karen Tsujimoto, *Wayne Thiebaud* (San Francisco: San Francisco Museum of Modern Art, 1985), 131.

16. Thiebaud, quoted in Aschheim and Daubert, *Episodes*, 53.

17. Wayne Thiebaud, quoted in Michael Zakian, "Two and One-Half Cakes, 1972," in *Delicious Metropolis: The Desserts and Urban Scenes of Wayne Thiebaud* (San Francisco: Chronicle Books, 2019), 59.

18. Other artists Thiebaud admires have created similar small sketches on a page, including Piet Mondrian and, in his student days, Richard Diebenkorn.

19. Michel Foucault, *This Is Not a Pipe*, trans. James Harkness (Berkeley, CA: University of California Press, 1983), 16.

20. Thiebaud, quoted in Albright, "Scrambling Around," 86.

21. Wayne Thiebaud, quoted in Andrée Maréchal-Workman, "Wayne Thiebaud's Cityscapes," *Images and Issues* (Winter 1981–1982): 68.

22. Foucault, *This Is Not a Pipe*, 23–24.

23. Foucault, *This Is Not a Pipe*, 21.

24. John Coplans, "Circles of Styles on the West Coast," *Art in America* 52, no. 3 (June 1964): 28.

25. Thiebaud, "Lollipop Tree?"

26. Thiebaud, quoted in Dervaux, *Draftsman*, 145.

27. Thiebaud, quoted in Aschheim and Daubert, *Episodes*, 34.

28. Thiebaud, quoted in Aschheim and Daubert, *Episodes*, 57.

29. Clement Greenberg, "The 'Crisis' of Abstract Art," in *Clement Greenberg: The Collected Essays and Criticism*, vol. 4, *Modernism with a Vengeance, 1957–1969*, ed. John O'Brian (Chicago: University of Chicago Press, 1993), 179.

30. According to Karen Tsujimoto, Thiebaud came to know the work of the Italian Macchiaioli through books. Tsujimoto, *Wayne Thiebaud*, 30.

31. Thiebaud says, "If you want to paint thickly with acrylic, the brush strokes won't stand up like they do in oil. You can't get that kind of combing; with acrylics the top edges are round, as opposed to being sharp edged. It's a big difference." Thiebaud, quoted in Wollheim, "Wayne Thiebaud"; John Wilmerding, "Wayne Thiebaud: 'The Emperor of Ice Cream,'" in *Wayne Thiebaud*, by John Wilmerding (New York: Acquavella Galleries, 2012), 30.

32. Foucault, *This Is Not a Pipe*, 22.

33. Wayne Thiebaud, interview by Carol Mancusi-Ungaro, Artists Documentation Program, Whitney Museum of American Art, June 27, 2001.

34. Wayne Thiebaud, quoted in "Looking through Wayne's Eyes," in *Wayne Thiebaud*, by Suzanne Swarts et al. (Wassenaar, Netherlands: Voorlinden, 2018), 111; John Coplans, *Wayne Thiebaud* (Pasadena, CA: Pasadena Art Museum, 1968), 30; see A. Le Grace G. Benson and David H. R. Shearer, "An Interview with Wayne Thiebaud," *Leonardo* 2, no. 1 (January 1969): 70.

35. Margaretta Lovell, cited by Hearne Pardee, "Wayne Thiebaud with Hearne Pardee," *Brooklyn Rail* (March 2019).

36. Steven Nash describes "the magic by which paint transforms itself into the things being described and back into raw substance." Nash, "Unbalancing Acts," 35; Rachel Teagle notes Thiebaud's ability to cause "sign to merge with referent and resolve again back into sign." Rachel Teagle, "Presence from Absence: Wayne Thiebaud and the Future of Painting," in *Wayne Thiebaud: 1958–1968*, by Rachel Teagle et al. (Oakland: University of California Press,

2018), 31; Malcom Warner says "art imitates life imitating art." Malcolm Warner, "Condominium Ridge, 1978," in *Delicious Metropolis: The Desserts and Urban Scenes of Wayne Thiebaud* (San Francisco: Chronicle Books, 2019), 103.

37. Wayne Thiebaud, quoted in Constance Lewallen, "Interview with Wayne Thiebaud," *View* 6, no. 6 (Winter 1990): 17; Thiebaud, quoted in Aschheim and Daubert, *Episodes*, 39.

38. Thiebaud, quoted in Berkson, "Thiebaud on the Figure."

39. Wayne Thiebaud, quoted in Adam Gopnik, "An American Painter," in *Wayne Thiebaud: A Paintings Retrospective*, by Steven A. Nash and Adam Gopnik (San Francisco: Fine Arts Museums of San Francisco, 2000), 54.

40. Adam Gopnik, "The Art World: Window Gazing," *New Yorker*, April 29, 1991, 78.

1

THIEBAUD, SACRAMENTO, AND THE FANCY STUFF OF ART

Scott A. Shields

Much of what has made Wayne Thiebaud the artist he is today is traceable to Northern California and, more specifically, to the Sacramento region. Thiebaud first came to know the light, heat, agriculture, and middle-American ambiance of the latter in 1942, when Sacramento was much smaller and its surroundings more rural, and he has lived in the city most of his life. The artist acknowledges, "Sacramento gave me something essential."[1]

Thiebaud is not, however, a Sacramento native; he was born in Mesa, Arizona, on November 15, 1920. His parents, Morton J. and Alice Eugena Thiebaud, named him Morton Wayne, after his father, and called him Wayne. In Mesa, both parents worked, his father as a mechanic, his mother for the telephone company. Less than a year after Thiebaud was born, the family moved to Long Beach, California.

Thiebaud has fond early memories of Long Beach, which he remembers as being "quiet [and] rather small in feeling," with beautiful stretches of beach and a surrounding countryside of orchards and orange groves.[2] His father worked in various capacities as a mechanic, engineer, and inventor, and was a bishop for the Mormon Church, coming to the religion as an adult through his wife, a descendant of Mormon pioneers. Faith was an integral part of the family's life, and Thiebaud participated in church activities. He also liked singing and playing the harmonica and guitar.

In the early years of the Great Depression, the Thiebauds relocated to Huntington Park, near Los Angeles. In 1931, they moved again to southern Utah,

settling first in Hurricane and then, with other extended family members, buying a farm between St. George and Cedar City. Thiebaud went to school first in Hurricane and then in St. George. He also did his fair share of chores: "I plowed, harrowed, dug, and hitched up teams . . . and planted and harvested alfalfa, potatoes, corn, . . . and I loved it," he recalls.[3] Today, he acknowledges that his later agricultural landscapes have some foundation in this early experience with the land.

In early 1933, the Thiebauds lost their ranch and moved to St. George where, for a time, they lived in a hotel. Looking for work, Thiebaud's father returned to California, hoping to get a job as part of the cleanup efforts following the March 10 Long Beach earthquake, which caused significant damage throughout Southern California. The family followed shortly thereafter and resettled in Long Beach, where Thiebaud spent an academic year at Alexander Hamilton Junior High School.

In 1935, Thiebaud enrolled at Long Beach Polytechnic High School. Though few of the school's formal offerings interested him, he did like sports, music and theater, participating in Boy Scout activities,

River Intersection (detail, pl. 90), 2010

and drawing.[4] He especially liked cartooning, sending some of his efforts to magazines for potential publication. He also held a variety of student-type jobs, all of which seem manifest in the subject matter of his later paintings. "I was raised on the beach," Thiebaud explains. "Grew up in Long Beach, and I sold papers on the beach, was a lifeguard in high school. So the beach was, and is, very much a part of my memory and my actual experience."[5] Another one of his jobs was at Mile High and Red Hot, a café known for its stacked ice-cream cones and hot dogs.[6] There were also, Thiebaud remembers, "rows of pies."[7] He later became more involved in high school theatrical productions, not so much performing as creating scenery and working on the stage crew. One of his favorite responsibilities was to control the spotlight that followed the actors, which sparked his interest in halation, as the light of the spot was ringed with spectral hues.[8] A similar spotlight falls on some of his subjects today, most recently, his circus folk.

In the summer of 1936, Thiebaud worked as an apprentice in the animation department at Walt Disney Studios, serving as an "in-betweener," the person who would render the frames connecting the more important images.[9] He was there only three months before being fired for participating in union activities. "Payment was something like fourteen dollars a week," he remembers, "But . . . that wasn't so bad, 'cause I was learning things."[10] This experience, along with others, made him more socially conscious, and for a time he even considered becoming a union lawyer.

Shortly before graduating from high school in 1938, Thiebaud broke his back playing sports with friends and was forced to graduate in a cast. The next fall, he began attending classes at the Frank Wiggins Trade School in Los Angeles, learning skills in lettering/sign-painting, cartooning, and commercial art. At first, the school's teachers were reluctant to admit him, as they thought he was too inexperienced, but they relented after seeing his sketches. Though his training at the school had nothing to do with "art or any of that fancy stuff," it did provide practical, straightforward skills that the artist continues to employ.[11] One of the signs Thiebaud remembers painting was for a shoeshine parlor, an appropriate starting point for someone who became gifted at rendering footwear. Also beneficial were skills he learned in illustration and advertising. He remembers one "old-fashioned illustrator" who showed him "how to put a hat on a head, and how to . . . paint shoes, or draw shoes, so that you started with the sole."[12] He gained additional experience as a sign painter and showcard illustrator at Sears, Roebuck and Company.

Trying to Become a Painter

The "fancy stuff" of art was becoming increasingly important to Thiebaud, and he spent time at the library perusing books on cartooning and the lives of artists, including Van Gogh and Rembrandt. He also made a trip to The Huntington in San Marino, California, where he saw their important collection of eighteenth-century British portraits, including Thomas Gainsborough's *The Blue Boy* (c. 1770) and Thomas Lawrence's *Sarah Goodin Barrett Moulton: "Pinkie"* (1794), which made a significant impression. Firsthand experience came through working with artist Norman Hart, a plein air painter and friend of his father's, who had a framing and art shop in Long Beach. Hart took Thiebaud to Palm Springs to show him how to paint landscapes. Thiebaud remembers other desert painters there as well, with some selling paintings off the running boards of their automobiles.[13] Later, in Sacramento, he too tried to sell paintings out of his car.

Also during this time, Thiebaud worked a variety of jobs, including as a freelance cartoonist and as an usher for movie theaters, including the Rivoli in Long Beach, for which he illustrated an occasional promotional poster.[14] The hours he spent near the snack counter and in the lobby, which was decorated with promotional stills and movie placards, were impactful. Movie-house food such as candy, soda, and popcorn have all featured prominently in his work since then, as have masks, show girls, ticket-sellers, and other theater-related subjects.

In 1940, Thiebaud enrolled at Long Beach Junior College (now Long Beach City College), mostly, he confesses, to play sports and experience fraternity life. Lacking in commitment, he dropped out after an academic year, receiving credit only for athletics and a course in public speaking. For a short time, he worked as a welder and shipfitter on Terminal Island near Long Beach. He then enlisted in the United States Army Air Forces to become a pilot.

Beginning in 1942, Thiebaud was stationed at Mather Field (now Mather Air Force Base), southeast of Sacramento. He did not become a pilot as planned but ended up working in the Special Services Division as a graphic artist and cartoonist. Coming back from servicing airplanes, he remembers, "I looked in a Quonset hut and saw these guys all in their uniforms with ties, drawing and painting [navigation and safety posters, etc.]. . . . So I went and knocked on the door and a nice fella came over. . . . 'Are you interested in that?' I said, 'Yeah, certainly.' He said, 'Well, can you draw?' 'Sure,' I says, 'Well, I can do cartoons.'"[15] Thiebaud would go on to produce his own comic strip—Aleck—for Wing Tips, the base's newspaper, along with other illustration and design work both for the military and for Weinstock, Lubin, and Co., a local department store chain. It was also during this time that he met Sacramento native Patricia Patterson. They married in 1943, whereupon Thiebaud became stepfather to a daughter, Jill.

In 1945, the military transferred Thiebaud to Culver City, California. Prior to his departure, he exhibited at what was then the E. B. Crocker Art Gallery (now Crocker Art Museum), submitting two works to the Kingsley Art Club's twentieth-annual exhibition under his military title, Sgt. Wayne Thiebaud.[16] In Culver City, the Air Force had temporarily taken over a movie lot, Hal Roach Studios, known as "The Laugh Factory to the World" because of its production of comedies, though now less affectionately called "Fort Roach." There, under commanding officer Ronald Reagan, Thiebaud assisted in making maps of Japan as well as training and propaganda films. He was discharged later that year. That same December, he and Patricia welcomed daughter Twinka.

After a brief stint as an advertising artist in Los Angeles, Thiebaud spent part of 1946 in New York with his family, where he sought steady work as a freelance cartoonist. It was a difficult time, and money was scarce; Thiebaud remembers living in a flophouse for seventy-five cents a night. He found work with Fairchild Publications in the art department of Women's Wear Daily, though he was unable to break into cartooning as he had hoped. The family returned to California and settled briefly in Sacramento before moving on to Los Angeles. Thiebaud took a position in the advertising office at Universal-International Pictures, which consisted primarily of constructing sets for publicity photographs and designing movie posters. The company soon fired him for participating in a labor strike.

Thiebaud next accepted a job at Rexall Drug Company in Los Angeles, working as a layout designer in advertising and as the illustrator of a cartoon strip for Rexall Magazine. The job honed his skills in perspective and foreshortening and helped him learn to reduce compositions to their essentials in order to best communicate a clear message. It also led him to investigate the artistic sources behind his pursuits. "The more I got

Fig. 8. *Wayne Thiebaud with friend and fellow artist Robert Mallary at Allan Stone Gallery, New York*, early 1960s. Photograph by Betty Jean Thiebaud

interested in layout and design, the more I was led to those examples in fine art from which they derived," he explains. "The most interesting designs were influenced by Mondrian or Degas or Matisse. That revelation really transfixed me. I started drawing a lot and read continually about it and slowly decided . . . that I was going to try to become a painter."[17]

Beyond his work experience, Thiebaud's time at Rexall was pivotal, because it was there that he met liberal, intellectual artist Robert Mallary, who, according to Thiebaud, introduced him to the "world of the mind (fig. 8)."[18] Mallary encouraged Thiebaud to paint seriously, finish his education, and pursue fine art as a career. He was often critical of Thiebaud's early efforts, which at the time were influenced by the modified Cubism of artists such as Lyonel Feininger and John Marin, whose paintings Thiebaud knew from books, as well as by the paintings he saw locally by Southern California artists like Rico Lebrun and Eugene Berman.[19] "He [Mallary] was a mentor who tore apart what I did," Thiebaud recalls. "I welcomed it because I needed his criticism so desperately."[20] So important was their relationship that in May 1952, when the Thiebauds welcomed their third daughter, they named her Mallary Ann.

As Thiebaud focused increasingly on his artwork, he also began to submit work to exhibitions. In 1948, he participated in the Los Angeles Museum of History, Science and Art's annual exhibition *Artists of Los Angeles and Vicinity*. A year later, he exhibited in *Artists under Thirty-Three*, a show organized by the Los Angeles Art Association. In 1949, he left Rexall to pursue a path toward becoming a fine artist, enrolling at San José State College (today San José State University) through the GI Bill. He took studio classes in painting and printmaking, as well as education courses so that he could teach.

In 1949, Thiebaud contributed to the Kingsley Art Club's annual exhibition at the Crocker, winning second prize for a work called *City Patterns*. He exhibited annually in Kingsley shows for most of the next fifteen years, as it was one of the few consistent exhibition opportunities available in Sacramento after he resettled in the city in 1950. Doing whatever he could to get his work before the public, he also contributed to regional county fairs and to the California State Fair. He even mounted displays in the concession building at Sacramento's Starlite Drive-In.

Thiebaud returned to Sacramento now both because he had developed a fondness for the area and because the art department at the newly founded Sacramento State College (today California State University, Sacramento) was encouraging. The art faculty was small—including Tarmo Pasto, Paul Beckman, and Robert Else—and it needed students. To encourage Thiebaud to transfer, professors offered him academic credit for his work experience and portfolio, lessening the number of classes he had to take. Art classes were held in a converted barn near campus, though Thiebaud, for the most part, focused on art history, theory, and education.[21] The informality of the situation and the curriculum suited him, and it was during this time that he truly came to appreciate art history.[22] He received a bachelor of arts degree in 1951.

That same year, while simultaneously attending graduate school at Sacramento State, Thiebaud began teaching at Sacramento Junior College (now Sacramento City College). The position stretched him, as he not only taught courses in drawing and painting but also in the history of art, often learning particulars of the latter just ahead of his students. The approach worked well enough that he later offered art history courses in areas new to him, including pre-Columbian and Asian art. He also taught classes in television production and commercial art and oversaw the art club, stage productions, and yearbook. Additionally, as a graduate student at Sacramento State, he designed sets for the theater department and helped Beckman create a course in stage design. It was a busy but exciting time. One of his most significant accomplishments was his solo exhibition in 1951 at the E. B. Crocker Art Gallery: *Influences on a Young Painter— Wayne Thiebaud*, which opened in February. He also held shows that year at the California State Library and at the Contemporary Gallery in Sausalito.

The Crocker exhibition featured sixty works, including oils, watercolors, temperas, pastels, drawings, and lithographs. It was arranged to illustrate Thiebaud's methods as well as to indicate the artists then inspiring him. His pieces ranged from Cubist-inspired abstractions to a series of paintings and lithographs based on children's stories and nursery rhymes. Audience favorites among the oil paintings included *Pied Piper*, a modern-day piper leading children out of the slums; *The City*, a "sparkling" interpretation of a jammed intersection; *Warm Winter*, an urban view after a snowstorm; and *The Bell*, a synesthetic attempt to convey sound and motion. There were also portraits of daughters Jill (an oil) and Twinka (a drawing), along with a depiction of Diego Rivera (a drawing). Still lifes of fruit and flowers were included, as was a scene of circus tents, these

subjects foreshadowing what was to come. John C. Oglesby of the *Sacramento Bee* called Thiebaud a "conservative modernist," because most of the work retained identifiable subject matter.[23] The few nonrepresentational pieces, each simply titled *Composition*, included Thiebaud-written labels, which helped elucidate them. In a joint lecture on modern art with sculptor R. Alan Williams, who had a contemporaneous display, Thiebaud further explained that modern art consisted of many styles, not just nonobjective arrangements.[24]

During his many visits to the Crocker, Thiebaud was able to see important works of early California art on display, along with drawings and other works in storage. The latter was facilitated by his wife, who had a job at the museum as a gallery assistant and artwork cataloguer.[25] Some of Thiebaud's landscapes of cliffs and rock formations are descendants of paintings collected by founders E. B. and Margaret Crocker, including Thomas Hill's 1871 *Great Canyon of the Sierra, Yosemite*, just as his paintings of deli counters and smorgasbords bear some relationship to Samuel Marsden Brookes's 1862 *Still Life (The Larder)* (fig. 9). Thiebaud's painting *Buffet* (fig. 10), for instance, described by one writer as "the richness of middle-

Fig. 9. Samuel Marsden Brookes (American, b. England, 1816–1892), ***Still Life (The Larder)***, 1862. Oil on canvas, 34 x 44 in. Crocker Art Museum, E. B. Crocker Collection, 1872.655

Fig. 10. *Buffet*, 1972–1975. Oil on canvas, 48⅛ x 60⅛ in. San Francisco Museum of Modern Art, gift of Jon and Shanna Brooks, Los Angeles, in memory of Paul LeBaron Thiebaud

class larders . . . displayed heroically on a domestic stage," updates many of the same bountiful elements Brookes depicts in his California still life of vegetables and game.[26] William Hahn's 1872 *Market Scene, Sansome Street, San Francisco* (fig. 11) also offered Thiebaud a worthy prototype by capturing a busy San Francisco street almost exactly one hundred years before Thiebaud began to paint urban views of the same locale.

Thiebaud wrote his master's thesis on the "Causes, Effects, and Implications of Stylistic Changes in the Arts," an indication of how well he had come to know art history. He received his master of arts in art from Sacramento State in 1953.[27] The following year, after having taught at Sacramento Junior College for three years, he became chair of the art department. He held this position until 1956 and then again from 1958 to 1960. Also in 1954, he started a small film-production company, Patrician Films, which until the end of the decade produced educational art films for young audiences.[28] At the same time, he designed sets for local stage productions.

During summers, as he had since the beginning of the 1950s, Thiebaud designed and directed the annual art exhibitions for the California State Fair, working with other local artists, including Patrick Dullanty, Larry Foster, Gregory Kondos, Jack Ogden, and Mel Ramos (fig. 12).[29] He also helped design and illustrate state fair

Fig. 12. *Artists Mel Ramos* (left) *and Wayne Thiebaud installing art at the California State Fair & Exposition, Sacramento,* 1956. Photographer unknown

catalogues and, on occasion, depicted scenes of the fair itself. It was an inspirational training ground, both for the rides and buildings that Thiebaud portrayed, as well as for the candy, comfort foods, and Americana that would soon assume a central place in his work.

Even with all of this going on, Thiebaud still found time to make art, which included not only painting but sculpture and printmaking, though he rarely had time to focus completely on his own projects.[30] In 1956, he decided to take a year-long sabbatical in New York, where he could pursue his art, visit museums and galleries, and meet other artists he admired. Because the city was so expensive, he also worked for two advertising agencies there.

At night, Thiebaud sometimes visited the Eighth Street Club and Cedar Tavern, the frequent haunts of top New York artists and critics. He became acquainted with both, including artists Willem and Elaine de Kooning,

Fig. 11. William Hahn (American, b. Germany, 1829–1887), **Market Scene, Sansome Street, San Francisco**, 1872. Oil on canvas, 60 x 96½ in. Crocker Art Museum, E. B. Crocker Collection, 1872.411

Franz Kline, and Barnett Newman, as well as art writers Harold Rosenberg, Clement Greenberg, Thomas Hess, and Leo Steinberg.[31] What he found most surprising—and inspirational—was the openness and acceptance with which these artists and tastemakers talked about art history, which was often frowned upon by artists in California:

> They talked more about Rembrandt and Ingres and Vermeer. It was just shocking to hear someone like Franz Kline talking about Vermeer, until you thought about his work. And it was shocking to know how much [Willem] de Kooning liked Fairfield Porter, for instance. It was interesting to hear Barnett Newman extoll and be so ecstatic over the *Mona Lisa*, and what he would say about it! So this gave me a whole different access to a kind of creative process, in a sense, (an understanding) that they really were genuinely searching for what they felt substantially meant something. And tradition was very, very important to them. That changed my attitude in a way. I think I had submerged what I had been interested in, sort of covering it over with gestural tracks of what I thought was a kind of arty, manipulative series of relationships, and it missed the point.[32]

Thiebaud's New York sabbatical helped him develop ideas that would crystallize back in California, though it would take four years for them to do so. In the meantime, he searched for subjects and an approach that was meaningful. Willem de Kooning's advice proved constructive: "You should find something that you really feel genuine in terms of your experience. . . . All the influences of the art world can trip you up. And while it's very important to understand art history, it's . . . not so important to be interested in what's happening today."[33]

Other defining moments came in 1957, after Thiebaud returned to California. That September, he opened another solo show at the Crocker Art Gallery: *Thiebaud—Recent Works*, which included nineteen oils and watercolors that were concerned, in Thiebaud's words, with the effects of strong, moving light on "glittering objects and devices of man."[34] That same month, the Oakland Art Museum (now Oakland Museum of California) opened their groundbreaking exhibition *Contemporary Bay Area Figurative Painting*, a show that Thiebaud went to see. This show celebrated artists reengaging with the visible world, which in California started with artist David Park, who disposed of his own Abstract Expressionist paintings and began adapting gestural brushwork to human figures and other subjects. Artists Elmer Bischoff and Richard Diebenkorn ultimately followed suit, these three artists and nine others included in the Oakland exhibition (fig. 13).[35] Thiebaud made sketches of some of the works on view, Bischoff's and Diebenkorn's paintings being especially impactful, as evidenced in his own paintings that followed, including *The Sea Rolls In* (1958; pl. 2) and *Zither Player* (1959; pl. 3). Diebenkorn's ideas, quoted in the Oakland catalogue, were also valuable: "One wants to see the artifice of the thing as well as the subject. Reality has to be digested, it has to be transmuted by paint. It has to be given a twist of some kind."[36] It was guidance that Thiebaud took to heart.

In 1958, Thiebaud helped found Sacramento's Artists Cooperative Gallery (ACG; later Artists Contemporary Gallery) with friends and became the gallery's first director.[37] That same year, he traveled to Mexico with some of the ACG artists, visiting art schools and looking at contemporary work made there. Also in 1958, he received an important commission from the Sacramento Municipal Utility District (SMUD) to create a mosaic mural for the exterior of its new, modernist headquarters. Having learned to compose on a grand scale by designing theater sets, he created *Water City* (pl. 4), which when finished would be 15 feet high and 250 feet long and wrap three sides of the building's ground floor.[38] The mural drew upon Pointillism, Cubism, and Abstract Expressionism to depict a colorful, confetti-like city set between a white river and sky. Thiebaud's handling of the buildings related to his state fair scenes, as well as to his jam-packed shop windows, all of which showcase dappled, transient light effects drawn from sources as disparate as Byzantine mosaics (the paintings sometimes even including metallic paint or leaf) and the paint splatters of Abstract Expressionism.[39] Other Thiebaud paintings and prints from the period depict similar clusters of activity and color set against pale expanses, making them compositional and chromatic progenitors—though far more frenzied—of his quieter still lifes soon to come.

Fig. 13. Richard Diebenkorn (American, 1922–1993), **Woman by a Large Window**, 1957. Oil on canvas, 70⅞ x 64⅞ in. Allen Memorial Art Museum, Oberlin, Ohio, R. T. Miller Jr. Fund, 1958, 1958.118. Courtesy of the Richard Diebenkorn Foundation

Digesting Reality

Thiebaud was in transition, both professionally and personally. In August 1958, he divorced Patricia. In December of the following year, he married Betty Jean Carr, becoming stepfather to her son Matt Bult and having a second son with her, Paul, the next October. The newlyweds honeymooned in Mexico, a trip that prompted Thiebaud to reengage with the beach as a subject. Looking at historical beach paintings, he found a worthy source of inspiration in the Spanish Impressionist Joaquín Sorolla. What proved more important than Sorolla's subject matter, however, was the artist's ability to capture water, light, and air with a bright bravura that could summarize an abundance of information in a confident brushstroke or two.

|29|

Fig. 14. David Park (American, 1911–1960), **Bathers**, 1956. Oil on canvas, 48 x 52 in. Private collection

Fig. 15. **Beach Boys**, 1959. Oil on canvas, 24 x 30 in. Thiebaud Family Collection

Work by the Bay Area Figurative painters, who also depicted bathers and people at the beach, factored in as well. Some of David Park's paintings provided direct inspiration, his scene of two male bathers heading into the surf (fig. 14) relating closely to both Thiebaud's *The Sea Rolls In* (1958; pl. 2) and the subsequent *Beach Boys* (1959; fig. 15). Though Thiebaud's works are closely related in subject and date, they evidence his rapid evolution. There is more Abstract Expressionism in the earlier painting, which is gestural and energetic, using

bold white swaths to indicate the crashing surf. *Beach Boys*, by contrast, is quieter, its brushstrokes smaller and more focused, and its color higher-keyed—all hallmarks of Thiebaud's emerging mature style.

In 1959, Thiebaud accepted a position as assistant professor in the Department of Art at the University of California, Davis, and began teaching in 1960.[40] The department was young, having started under Richard L. Nelson, who taught art practice beginning in 1952 in what was then the Department of Philosophy and Fine

Arts. Studio artists Roland Petersen and Ralph Johnson joined the faculty in 1956 and 1957 respectively, and then, in 1958, Nelson became chair of what would henceforward be an independent Department of Art. Nelson subsequently hired Thiebaud, Tio Giambruni (1961), William Wiley (1962), Jane Garritson (1963), Roy De Forest (1965), and Manuel Neri (1965). In 1962, Robert Arneson, Ruth Horsting, and Daniel Shapiro transferred from the School of Home Economics, adding to a pool of professorial art talent that could hardly be matched anywhere.

There was a great deal of freedom in teaching at Davis, and most of the faculty had little formal experience as educators, meaning that their methods varied widely.[41] Because most of the artists were doing well professionally (several would ultimately show in New York), there was more camaraderie than competition. Thiebaud felt "lucky" to be in this atmosphere, with its "close associations, [and] a lot of admiration for each other."[42] According to Ralph Johnson, "It was like catching the right boat at the right time. The place took off."[43]

The artists were also brought together by the fact that many of them relied on humor as part of their aesthetic. Funk, Pop, Dude Ranch Dada, Nut Art, and other labels have been variously applied to describe the irreverent wit and California attitude manifested at Davis. In addition to Thiebaud, whose humor was wry and subtle, faculty members such as Arneson, de Forest, and Wiley became known for the subversive comedy of their art, and visiting instructors—including Clayton Bailey, David Gilhooly, and Peter Saul—did too. Plus, there were numerous witty and talented students who trained there, especially in the realm of ceramics under Arneson.[44] There were certainly also visiting instructors at Davis of more serious persuasion, among them William Theophilus Brown, Gordon Cook, Elaine de Kooning, Robert Mallary, Don Nice, Joseph Raffael,

Fig. 16. *Artist Robert Arneson, UC Davis Chancellor James Meyer, Wayne Thiebaud, and artist Harvey Himelfarb* (left to right) *at the University of California, Davis*, n.d. Photographer unknown

Paul Waldman, and Paul Wonner. Thiebaud shared friendships—and frequently aesthetic concerns—with these artists as well.

Nearby Sacramento State College also had its share of artist-humorists. Mel Ramos, having earlier been Thiebaud's student at Sacramento Junior College, earned his bachelor of arts and master of arts from that institution before going on to receive recognition for paintings of comic-book heroes and female nudes playfully paired with oversized objects. Chicagoans Jim Nutt and Gladys Nilsson came to Sacramento State to teach in 1968, bringing their outrageous "Hairy Who" style with them. Several Nutt/Nilsson students incorporated comedy into their own work, with some continuing to do so today.

Thiebaud believes there is a place for humor in art, and he's pleased when people view his paintings and smile. His wit is generally more understated and tongue-in-cheek than many of his colleagues listed above, Thiebaud's having to do with caricature and the redefinition of ordinary things or actions through scale, color, space, and light—tricks he learned as a layout artist.[45] Caricature, as Thiebaud uses it, introduces humor as it distorts, emphasizing some elements and deemphasizing others. A means of playing with reality, it is an assembly of little white lies that somehow arrives at the truth.

In May 1960, Thiebaud sent out an invitation to his solo exhibition at the Nut Tree in Vacaville, California, which acknowledged his then current—and still primarily formal—artistic concerns: "At present I am interested in the more transitory properties of light and what it does to the color and shape of people and things."[46] The Nut Tree's design director, Don Birrell, former director of the E. B. Crocker Art Gallery and curator of Thiebaud's 1951 show there, arranged for the exhibition at the Nut Tree complex, which in addition to a small gallery included a restaurant, bakery, candy counter, coffee shop, gift store, toy shop, and even a miniature Nut Tree Railroad connecting to a functioning Nut Tree Airport. Though an unusual venue for Thiebaud's work, the foods served at the complex's restaurant and candy shop certainly paralleled those in the still lifes that he would start experimenting with later that fall, when his art began its profound aesthetic and conceptual shift.

In Thiebaud's first signature paintings of desserts and other foods and common objects, his subjects were rather incidental to his formal experiments with shape and volume. In fact, his iconography did not change all that much, as he had been painting middlebrow subjects like food counters, slot and pinball machines, and window displays since 1953. In these earlier works, however, his expressive paint application camouflaged and diminished the impact of his subjects, which was by intent, as he was conflicted about whether subject matter should be there in the first place. By his own admission the paintings were "articulated and hyped up with Abstract Expressionist brush strokes," which he hoped might make them look like art.[47] He now sought to paint with greater clarity and precision, and in a style more uniquely his own. He remembers the moment and his thought process:

> What am I going to paint? I decided since I'd been using every mannerism I could think of, and all this . . . why don't I just try to get a composition as basic as I can, see if I can get the planes to sit properly, the space to work properly. What shall I paint? Well, I am going to take basic shapes: a triangle, a rectangle, some squares or parallelograms or whatever architecture I can think of, and I made these ovals thinking I am going to put something on those and see if I can make them sit on those things. And triangles went on them and I thought to myself, "Let's see, I have worked in a lot of restaurants and I've seen rows of pies and things." So when I got these ovals and put these triangles, I made sort of basic pies. I just made it very plain at first, and I had not realized what I had done. . . . I ended up with this row of pie paintings and stupefied myself. I mean, I virtually said to myself, "That would be the end of a serious painter."[48]

Thiebaud's arrival at this moment was due, in part, to the work and lessons of French Post-Impressionist Paul Cézanne. Not only was there the general influence that Cézanne's still lifes held, but also significant was the master's ability to combine the Impressionist immediacy of vision with a new emphasis on volume and weight. "In Cézanne['s work]," Thiebaud explains, "there is always this swelling, like the volume trying to get away from the plane, even though there is also a linear matrix. It's like trying to have both worlds simultaneously."[49] Thiebaud was grappling with similar formal concerns—and at an equally pivotal moment. He, too, was reintroducing three-dimensional solidity into his paintings, which had all but been expunged by the Abstract Expressionists' concern with surface. Like Cézanne's divergence from the Impressionists, Thiebaud was transgressing the boundaries set by the preceding generation.

Cézanne advocated his own approach in a letter to artist Émile Bernard, his advice quoted in a locally authored book of importance to Thiebaud: Erle Loran's *Cézanne's Composition: Analysis of His Form with Diagrams and Photographs of His Motifs*. In it, Loran quoted Cézanne: "One must first of all study geometric forms: the cone, the cube, the cylinder, the sphere. When one knows how to render these things in their form and their planes, one ought to know how to paint."[50] In his early mature still lifes, one can almost feel Thiebaud listening to this advice, finding Cézanne's cones, cubes, cylinders, and spheres in food and other everyday products that lent themselves to abstraction. Layer cakes are, after all, cylinders; ice-cream cones are cones and spheres, gumballs and gumball machines are also spheres; and deli counters, pinball, and slot machines are variations on the cube. The selection of informal subjects for formal experimentation became, as writer Adam Gopnik has described, "the essential Thiebaud aesthetic: highly simplified geometric forms, squares and cylinders and rectangles and cubes, taken from the most unpretentious vernacular form and painted with a dense, textured, dancing richness."[51]

Just as he was starting to find his voice, Thiebaud got another dose of Diebenkorn through the exhibition *Recent Paintings by Richard Diebenkorn*, which was on view at San Francisco's California Palace of the Legion of Honor from October 22 to November 27, 1960. "I remember sitting and looking at them [Diebenkorn's paintings]," he later explained, "and feeling a number of things, and thinking 'I have to see these more clearly.' I sat for quite a few hours and made diagrammatic, rather careful, analytic, schematic drawings of the work, and learnt a great deal about its character."[52] What Thiebaud appreciated most was the straightforwardness of Diebenkorn's paintings, which felt fresh, "not fussed with or modified . . . a beautiful direct encounter."[53] It was an experience that confirmed and fostered the changes taking place in Thiebaud's own work.

While Thiebaud's depictions of pie may have started out as formal exercises in rendering basic forms and shapes, he nevertheless admits to selecting his unassuming subject because he had not often seen it portrayed. "I've seen Brueghel's pies, and Chardin's fruits and so on, but . . . there wasn't a lot of that."[54] Other food subjects were equally colloquial, many of them in shapes similar to pie on plates, including sandwiches cut into wedges and triangular slices of watermelon. Edibles other than desserts were generally less conducive to Thiebaud's love of simultaneity than were custard, meringue, frosting, and ice cream, though this does not mean that the paintings lacked expressive paint handling. His *Watermelon Slices* (1961), for instance, is very painterly overall, the brushwork continuing the approach pursued by Bay Area Figuratives such as Diebenkorn, though the impasto is mainly in the background rather than in the watermelon's rind and flesh, with which it is less compatible. The same is true of his 1961 *Hamburger* (pl. 6), the "empty" spaces boasting most of the attention-seeking strokes of paint.

Though many of Thiebaud's foods are serially repeated, others, like his *Hamburger*, are presented as meals. There are breakfasts of bacon and eggs, pancakes and coffee, and a box and bowl of cereal (pl. 5). There are also sandwich-and-hamburger lunches and truck-stop suppers. The latter consisted of meat, fries, slices of white bread, and a glass of milk. The choice of milk—as opposed to a soda or beer—was pure Thiebaud, connoting a middle-American innocence, along with, perhaps, a bit of conservatism leftover from his Mormon upbringing. Though paintings like these were certainly unusual, they were not unprecedented. In California in the 1930s, for instance, Armin Hansen depicted leftover dishes in *After Lunch* and *After Dinner*; George Kennedy Brandriff depicted a meal about to begin in *Sunday Breakfast* (fig. 17). Bay Area Figurative painter Joan Brown rendered a *Thanksgiving Turkey* in 1959 (fig. 18), a painterly progenitor to Thiebaud's 1961 *Barbecued Chickens* (fig. 19) set forth unceremoniously in an enamel pan.

To Thiebaud, his new still-life paintings were the "most genuine" work he had yet done, as they seemed to communicate some of his life experience.[55] Although he would persist in paying close attention to his subjects' formal qualities and how they might lend themselves to object transference, he also consciously chose them for their potential resonance with a broad—and specifically American—audience. He explained his rationale: "I remember thinking also about being an American and growing up in America, loving all kinds of painting, but somehow where I came from, what I have really experienced, to stay with that, because that felt good, that felt real to me."[56]

Thiebaud's foods are ubiquitous, the type served at snack counters, cafeterias, and middle-class diners across the United States. They are foods most Americans have eaten and, on average, can afford. Thiebaud has been careful to paint "good old American" cakes and pies, though he could just as easily have portrayed more elegant European desserts.[57] He has been equally cognizant about the meanings that other foods carry: American sandwich bread as opposed to a French baguette, for example. Such simple fare was not only

Fig. 17. George Kennedy Brandriff (American, 1890–1936), **Sunday Breakfast**, c. 1935. Oil on canvas, 24 x 30 in. The Buck Collection at the UCI Museum and Institute of California Art

Fig. 18. Joan Brown (American, 1938–1990), **Thanksgiving Turkey**, 1959. Oil on canvas, 47⅞ x 47⅞ in. Museum of Modern Art, New York, Larry Aldrich Foundation Fund, 80.1960 © The Museum of Modern Art / Licensed by SCALA / Art Resource, NY

American, it was nostalgic, evoking simpler times and places. "It's just very, very *familiar*," he explains. "I spent time in food preparation, I sold papers on the streets, and I went into Kresses or Woolworths or Newberrys, to see the eccentric display of peppermint candy. They're mostly painted from memory—from memories of bakeries and restaurants—any kind of window display . . . there's a lot of yearning there."[58]

Sacramento was the perfect place for such a pursuit, as the city was—and is—much like communities in the agricultural Midwest, despite being located in California. This was especially true in the 1950s and early 1960s when, as Thiebaud recalls, Sacramento "was still a very American place with its old cafeterias, streetcars, people dressed up."[59] The food was also not much different from that found elsewhere, a sameness that Thiebaud sought to exploit:

> I looked for things that I thought were sort of anonymous. Pies, and particularly pie-cases, displays; and going across the country it did occur to me that wherever you went, you could almost always see the same kind of pie counter, the same kind of hamburger, the same kind of Boston cream. So what do you do about that? I wasn't interested in just *presenting* it. How do you take a visual cliché and imbue it with vibrancy?[60]

At first, it seems, Thiebaud does "just present" his subjects, as he lays them out with such deadpan banality. He also assigns innocuous titles that simply confirm—and sometimes count—the things he presents: *Two Pies* (1961), *Five Hot Dogs* (1961), *Four Pinball Machines* (1962). This contradicts the often literal sweetness of the subjects themselves, as do the stark environments into which he places them, which helps

Fig. 19. ***Barbecued Chickens***, 1961. Oil on canvas, 19 x 24 in. Private collection

keep the paintings from becoming visual clichés. In his early artist's statement, Thiebaud acknowledged wanting to convey a sense of our "stainless steel, porcelain, enameled, plastic world," a goal that has fostered a compelling tension with his oft-nostalgic iconography.[61] It is a dichotomy between genuineness and artificiality that he had known for a long time—back to his days of working in movie theaters, at Walt Disney and Universal-International Pictures, in advertising, and at the California State Fair.

Thiebaud has stated that what makes a good or bad painting has nothing to do with social commentary.[62] And yet, there is no denying the presence of social commentary in what he decides to include or leave out. He readily admits to making selections for their "telltale evidence of what we're about as a people or as a society."[63] His early artist's statement admitted his desire to evoke "rather obvious notions about conformism, mechanized living, and mass produced culture."[64]

To him, this was not only acceptable but desirable, because it was part of what made his art an honest reflection of his time and place:

> We are hesitant to make our own life special, . . . set our still lifes aside, . . . applaud or criticize what is especially us. We don't want our still lifes to tattle on us. But some years from now our foodstuffs, our pots, our dress, and our ideas will be quite different. So if we sentimentalize or adopt a posture more polite than our own we are not having a real look at ourselves for what we are.[65]

The Slice-of-Cake School

By the spring of 1961, Thiebaud produced what he felt were enough good paintings to warrant a new exhibition. That May and June, he held a show of recent work at the Artists Cooperative Gallery in Sacramento. In December, he held another at Art Unlimited in San Francisco. Neither garnered much attention. In between these exhibitions, he set off for New York to try to secure a venue there. Traveling on a university fellowship with his family during the summer, he made inquiries at numerous galleries but was uniformly declined. He did not initially call on Allan Stone, the man who would become his longtime dealer, as he was told by Robert Mallary that Stone wasn't interested in his work. Just as he was about to give up and return to Sacramento, however, Mallary's wife urged Thiebaud to give Stone a try.[66]

At first, Stone was not entirely convinced of the merits of Thiebaud's paintings, though he was compelled enough to agree to a show. It was a personal risk, as he had not been in business very long, and thus he started by including just a single Thiebaud food painting in a group show that December. By April, however,

Stone had worked up the "courage" for a major presentation: *Wayne Thiebaud: Recent Paintings*, which opened on April 17, 1962.[67] Although Thiebaud had exhibited in the city previously at Staempfli Gallery, this was his first New York presentation of mature work.

Featuring pies, layer cakes, cupcakes, ice-cream sundaes, lollipops, pastry and deli counters, syrup dispensers, lunch counters, hamburgers, barbequed chickens and ribs, and pinball and slot machines, the exhibition was successful to a degree that neither Thiebaud nor Stone could have anticipated. Many influential artists, collectors, and critics came to see and write about the show, and every single piece sold. Reviews and articles appeared in newspapers such as the *New York Times* and *New York Post*, as well in journals and magazines like *Art International*, *Art News*, *Artforum*, *Life*, and *The Nation*. *Time* magazine even credited Thiebaud with creating a "slice-of-cake school."[68] Architect Philip Johnson and critic Max Kozloff bought paintings for themselves, and the Museum of Modern Art in New York and the Wadsworth Atheneum in Hartford, Connecticut, acquired pieces for their permanent collections.[69] Stone would give Thiebaud a solo show almost every year thereafter until the dealer's death in 2006.

In hindsight, the exhibition was perfectly timed, as it coincided exactly with a watershed moment in the art world. Three years after the fact, the era's preeminent art critic, Clement Greenberg, recognized the significance of the moment:

> In the spring of 1962 there came the sudden collapse, market-wise and publicity-wise, of Abstract Expressionism as a collective manifestation. The fall of that year saw the equally sudden triumph of Pop art, which, though deriving its vision from the art of [Robert]

Rauschenberg and especially [Jasper] Johns, is much more markedly opposed to painterly abstraction in its handling and general design.[70]

Thiebaud's show, happening as it did in the spring of 1962, was not just on the cutting edge, it was ahead of it. And yet, Thiebaud was not, as Greenberg stated, opposed to painterly abstraction in perhaps the same way that other Pop artists were. Kozloff, of *The Nation*, noted this in his review of Thiebaud's work, referring to the artist's paint application as a union of form and content that was neither naturalism nor abstraction. The reviewer also interpreted the paintings as containing "significant commentary on contemporary mass culture."[71] Thomas B. Hess of *Art News* and sculptor Donald Judd, writing for *Arts Magazine*, were even more decisive about the latter point. Hess stated that Thiebaud "preaches revulsion by isolating the American food habit."[72] Judd decided that the main point was the "existential nausea of innumerable things," describing Thiebaud's painting of cupcakes aligned in six rows as a "gross army," yet he liked the paintings overall.[73] Thiebaud himself, however, saw what he was doing as more observational than satirical, stating matter-of-factly, "At present I am painting still lifes taken from window displays, store counters, supermarket shelves, and mass produced items from manufacturing concerns in America."[74]

Though most critics were accepting and even laudatory of this new populist trend, Greenberg was skeptical, as he had long championed art that was purely formal in its concerns. His article "After Abstract Expressionism" appeared in *Art International* in the fall of 1962, after several artists of the Pop persuasion, Thiebaud included, had their first solo shows in New York. Though Greenberg did not mention Thiebaud by name, he was clearly thinking of him when he described

artists who depicted "plucked chickens instead of dead pheasants, or coffee cans, or pieces of pastry instead of flowers in vases." Though not enamored of such subjects, Greenberg did not object to the approach: "Not that I do not find the clear and straightforward academic handling of their pictures refreshing after the turgidities of Abstract Expressionism; yet the effect is only momentary, since novelty, as distinct from originality, has no staying power."[75] Today, it seems safe to say that Greenberg was wrong about Pop's longevity.

Thiebaud's New York show closed on May 5, 1962. Two months later, the M. H. de Young Memorial Museum in San Francisco opened *An Exhibition of Paintings by Wayne Thiebaud*, some of the paintings having been shown previously with Stone. Late that September, his work was also included in the groundbreaking exhibition *New Painting of Common Objects* at the Pasadena Art Museum (now the Norton Simon Museum), which is today considered the first group exhibition of Pop Art in the United States for bringing now-canonical artists together, such as Jim Dine, Joe Goode, Roy Lichtenstein, Edward Ruscha, and Andy Warhol. Just as this exhibition closed, a related one opened in New York at Sidney Janis Gallery: *International Exhibition of the New Realists*. It too included Thiebaud's work alongside key figures like Warhol and Lichtenstein, as well as Christo, Claes Oldenburg, Tom Wesselmann, and others.

Although the artists in these exhibitions had striking commonalities, especially in their subject matter, *Time* magazine described this as more of a coincidence than reciprocal influence: "Unknown to one another, a group of painters have come to the common conclusion that the most banal and even vulgar trappings of modern civilization can, when transposed literally to canvas, become Art."[76] And yet, for Thiebaud (both then and now), the association felt misaligned with his

true concerns: "I didn't think of myself as a Pop artist. So I continued to explore what I thought were, pretty much, formal realist problems from my perspective, even though they were things which were common objects."[77]

Thiebaud's approach was distinct from artists like Warhol and Lichtenstein, who favored a more mechanical look and means of paint application. Though Thiebaud depicted common—and sometimes mass-produced—objects, he did not want his paintings to appear machine-made: "One of the responsibilities of the serious painter, it seems to me," he explains, "is to . . . ensure that each completed painting is not a repetitive manufactured product, but a unique and independent work."[78] Warhol, by contrast, silkscreened his Campbell's Soup cans, Coca-Cola bottles, and celebrity portraits, effacing his own role in the process; Lichtenstein's Ben-Day dots sacrificed painting in favor of a "mass-produced" comic-book style that linked the artist and the machine. In his early review of Thiebaud, Judd took note of the difference, stating, "Lichtenstein uses the schema of commercial representation which stops with itself, unlike the technique communicative of the object which Thiebaud uses."[79]

Whereas both Warhol's and Lichtenstein's work projected an air of impersonal detachment, Thiebaud's paintings, being labored over and loved, manifest evidence of the artist's hand, making them decidedly personal and, by extension, more inherently optimistic. This does not imply that his paintings fail to critique consumerism and the isolation one can feel even in a world of abundance. They do. And yet, in their care and undeniable reverence for painting, they are also celebratory, validating art, the role of the artist, and—for better or worse—our contemporary world. This pessimistic/optimistic dichotomy is in part responsible for providing Thiebaud's simple subjects with their enduring interest, though it has taken many years and a large

body of work for reviewers and critics to come to terms with the incongruity of his intent. In 1962, for instance, Brian O'Doherty of the New York Times interpreted Thiebaud's paintings as cynical, comparing them to Edward Hopper's scenes and writing that both artists imparted a "comfortable desolation of much American life."[80] By 2012, however, Pepe Karmel identified just the opposite: "Thiebaud's painted vision of a meaningful, fundamentally beneficent world sets him at odds with his contemporaries, who are more likely to remind us of the anxiety and alienation that often seem to characterize modern life."[81]

Also setting Thiebaud's work apart from that of many Pop artists is its fully realized three-dimensionality. In the 1950s, Thiebaud's own paintings were flat and his imagery obscured. With a new decade he punctured the picture plane with perspectival recession, volumetric form, and shadow. It was a departure from the Abstract Expressionists, who considered the sanctity of the picture plane inviolable, and, to a slightly lesser degree, the Bay Area Figuratives, who rendered imagery but with an Abstract Expressionist surface. Jasper Johns provided a link between Abstract Expressionism and the new generation of Pop artists by combining the former's distinctive paint handling with recognizable imagery that was flat to begin with—such as flags, targets, numbers, and maps. Rauschenberg also appropriated flat, media-inspired imagery; Robert Indiana's text pieces generally stayed true to the picture plane; and Warhol and Lichtenstein's graphic imagery remained surface-oriented as well. In their illusionistic three-dimensionality, Thiebaud's paintings had more in common with the inherently three-dimensional sculpture of Oldenburg, which, at the time, was also handmade in appearance. In addition, Oldenburg's subject matter was strikingly parallel, including pieces such as Pastry Case, I (1961–1962; fig. 20);

Cold Cereal (detail, pl. 5), 1961

Floor Cake (1962); and *Floor Cone* (1962), which, like Thiebaud's works, were similarly imbued with a subtle humor. Dine's subjects, including doughnuts, tools, and neckties, were also related in selection and wit.

Thiebaud, Oldenburg, and Dine were also less likely than other artists of the era to appropriate imagery directly from commercial advertising and packaging. For Thiebaud, having worked in the commercial realm, it was a matter of respect for graphic artists' individuality and skill. "Illustrators, cartoonists, graphic designers, sign painters—they're all heroes to me," he defends.[82] And yet, at the same time, Thiebaud's paintings do relate to advertising—especially 1940s and '50s advertising—even if they are not unapologetic appropriations. An ad for Betty Crocker's Country Kitchen Recipe Cake Mixes, for instance, shows slices of cake lusciously hand-frosted, three-dimensional, and receding into space (fig. 21). All the pieces are similar and of the same size, though each is also distinct. Thiebaud's desserts, likewise, retain their own "uniqueness and specialness," even when regimented in rows.[83] Had Warhol been inclined to take on cake, by contrast, the result would surely have resembled an ad for Swans Down Cake Mix, which depicts multiple, commercially designed cake-mix boxes in flat, serialized repetition (fig. 22).

These essential differences are what led Allan Stone to appreciate Thiebaud's work over Warhol's. The gallerist explained, "There was something about [Warhol's] work that was a little flat for me. . . . I liked the kind of surface and the lushness [of Thiebaud's work]. . . . You sense a love of paint and surface, . . . there's a real joy of painting, a joy of life in his work."[84] Thiebaud himself appreciates these same qualities: "There is a long tradition of painting that I happen to admire, in which the paint is obviously manipulated by hand. That kind of coding and descriptive characteristics [are] very fundamental to my inquiry."[85] The significance of Thiebaud's

brushwork cannot be overstated. Combed passages animate otherwise empty expanses; thick areas of pigment mimic actual substances and add dimensionality; smooth sections create push-and-pull against areas that stand proud in relief. All of this, the artist hopes, will bestow his surfaces with a "life-force."[86]

Thiebaud's abundant use of white also helps create the perception that his paintings emit their own energy—and light. Adam Gopnik describes the light in Thiebaud's paintings as manifesting "the sudden glare" of the West Coast, "just after you take off your sunglasses."[87] Such light could certainly be felt in Thiebaud's childhood home of Long Beach, where the sun reflects off the sea, but it is also omnipresent in Sacramento, where light radiates heat. Author Jack Kerouac, in his book *On the Road*, noted the contrast between California's light and landscape and that of states in the East. "There is something brown and holy about the East," Kerouac's Sal Paradise decided, "and California is white like washlines."[88] Thiebaud's paintings often include an abundance of "washline" white, though the artist prefers to describe white as being like "Chardin tablecloths," in that it is composed of all colors and both absorbs and reflects light.[89]

Some of the strongest and deepest colors in Thiebaud's paintings are to be found in his shadows, which he studied under Sacramento's scorching sun, finding that strong sunlight on shadows creates different colors at their edges than at their centers.[90] The same is true of strong interior lighting, especially fluorescent lighting, which Thiebaud appreciates because it connotes the "starkness and glare" and "air-conditioned atmosphere" of the contemporary world that he aims to capture.[91] He explains, "Today the idea of light is tremendously variable. Strong display lights have been developed which can . . . make an object cast colored shadows, change its local color before your eyes, glow and develop a halo or imbue it with a

Fig. 20. Claes Oldenburg (American, b. Sweden, 1929), **Pastry Case, I**, 1961–1962. Burlap and muslin soaked in plaster, painted with enamel, metal bowls, and ceramic plates in glass-and-metal case, 20¾ x 30⅛ x 14¾ in. Museum of Modern Art, New York, The Sidney and Harriet Janis Collection, 639.1967.a-dd © The Museum of Modern Art / Licensed by SCALA / Art Resource, NY

Fig. 21. **Advertisement for Betty Crocker's Country Kitchen Recipe Cake Mixes**, 1959

Fig. 22. **Advertisement for Swans Down Cake Mix**, 1955

pulsating effect."[92] In his paintings, this translates into colorful halations that enwreathe his subjects and add vibrancy. At the same time, they transition objects or people into stark environments, "so the eye will accept the form as not being so pasted on."[93]

Human Enterprises

Because Thiebaud did not want to become pigeon-holed as a still-life painter, he successfully applied for a grant from the University of California, Davis, that allowed him to take time off from teaching and to paint life-sized figures.[94] He pursued this endeavor over the course of the 1964–1965 academic year, learning quickly that depictions of people were not as forgiving as still lifes, because viewers are more acutely attuned to the human body. "I think it's the *most* important study there is," Thiebaud states, "and the most challenging and the most difficult."[95] At first, Thiebaud tried to work from memory, as he had in his still lifes, though the results were unsuccessful. He then turned to models, which helped him get the facts right. He started with friends and family, who would pose patiently and for free; he later hired models.

Thiebaud generally placed his sitters in vacant white or neutral spaces, which along with strong lighting, forced viewers to focus on the person, not their environment. His early experience constructing sets for publicity photographs at Universal-International Pictures informed his approach, as did, perhaps, trends in fashion photography, which he knew about from his stint at *Women's Wear Daily*. As with his still lifes, Thiebaud surrounded his figures with halations of color to enliven and counterbalance the stasis of their poses and to connect them with the surrounding space.

Many have described Thiebaud's figurative paintings as human "still lifes," as his subjects do not reveal their feelings or engage the viewer. It is an assessment that the artist has affirmed: "The isolated figure series . . . [is] not supposed to reveal anything. . . . It's like seeing a stranger in some place like an airline terminal for the first time. You look at him. You notice his shoes, his suit, the pin in his lapel, but you don't have any particular feeling about him."[96] Thiebaud achieved this sense of distance and reserve even though he was on intimately familiar terms with most of his early subjects. Betty Jean, who posed for several of her husband's most iconic figure paintings, fully understood that she would be reduced to "objectness," inanimate like any other subject caught in a frozen moment of time.[97]

Thiebaud was careful not to pose his sitters in ways that might seem illustrational or evoke narrative, as part of the task he set for himself was to depict a person revealing nothing and doing nothing—just waiting for something to occur. As with his pie (selected in part because he had "never seen a pie painted"), he sought a new way of approaching the human form by capturing people in insignificant—and often liminal—moments.[98]

> Most people in figure paintings have always done something. The figures have been standing posing, fighting, loving, and what I'm interested in, really, is the figure that is about to do something, or has done something, or is doing nothing, and, with that sort of centering device, try to figure out what can be revealed, not only to people, but to myself.[99]

The results of depicting people "doing nothing" proved surprisingly illuminating. Rather than impede engagement and potential for meaning as one might expect, such self-conscious passivity invited viewers to draw upon their own experience to explain what the people portrayed might be thinking or feeling.

Sliced Circle (detail, pl. 49), 1986

Thiebaud would continue to paint figures off and on for the rest of his career, but in 1966 he changed his primary focus yet again, this time to landscape painting. As with portrayals of family and friends, he turned to scenes he knew well, selecting subjects from the Sacramento Valley, nearby foothills, and the Sierra Nevada. Driving east from Sacramento, the landscape transitions from flat, agricultural land and riverscapes into rocky hillsides and, shortly thereafter, exalted mountain terrain. Thiebaud drew and painted many of these scenes onsite, completing larger works back in his studio. Though he may have started with a recognizable source, he always manipulated the view in proportion, perspective, and color. He also often eliminated the horizon line, literally giving his landscapes an ungrounded quality meant to circumvent tradition and "throw people off."[100]

Many of Thiebaud's landscapes are almost entirely invented, drawing more from his imagination and memory than from nature. He also sought inspiration in non-traditional sources, such as George Herriman's comic strip *Krazy Kat*, the antics of which were often set in a fantastical southwestern landscape (fig. 33, p. 75). Thiebaud describes Herriman as a "big hero," just as the cartoonist was for Elmer Bischoff, Richard Diebenkorn, and others of the era, and admits that "a lot" of his own landscapes come out of *Krazy Kat*—"clouds, mesa, and things."[101] For Thiebaud, the introduction of humor and cartoon strategies into the long (and in California, especially, revered) tradition of landscape painting was one more way to breathe new life into an old subject. As Thiebaud put it, "Cartoons allow the silly to sit with the sublime."[102]

The dizzying height and unbalance of some of these landscapes led naturally to Thiebaud's cityscapes. He had painted city views before, including several related to his *Water City* mural, but these paintings had been more traditionally formatted. His new paintings were upright and precipitous, focusing on San Francisco's roller-coaster-like streets and buildings precariously perched on steep hills. Thiebaud began the series in the early 1970s after he bought a second home in San Francisco's Potrero Hill neighborhood, which lent itself to his new concerns. He began his investigations by painting more than twenty works from various intersections, hoping to capture the drama of the urban landscape.

Initially, Thiebaud had trouble obtaining the effects he desired, until critic Brian O'Doherty advised him that Edward Hopper produced city views from an amalgam of sketches assembled back in the studio. Thiebaud consequently stopped painting and started drawing, creating hundreds of sketches that he would ultimately revise and reconstruct, combining what he could see with what he wanted to convey: a synesthetic feeling or idea of the city that could affect viewers on a visceral level. It was, not coincidentally, the same dizzying effect that Alfred Hitchcock hoped to achieve when he selected San Francisco as the setting for his 1958 film *Vertigo*.

Thiebaud credits his uncle, a road-maker, with sparking his interest in cities at an early age. His uncle gave him toy bulldozers and cars and encouraged him to create a make-believe metropolis in the backyard. Ever since then, Thiebaud acknowledges, "I've remained interested in the city as a human enterprise, and the pile of human tracks it contains and the byways of living and moving."[103] Like his still lifes, the city is human-made and manipulated. There is also a sense of unfulfilled aspiration and isolation in its presentation. "Some have to do with longing and yearning for something unattainable, the urge to reach heights and build a fantasy world," he explains, "and some have to do with dirt and grit and the loneliness of the streets."[104]

The influence of Asian art is also apparent in these cityscapes, especially in Thiebaud's use of cropping and reversed perspectives. The multiple vanishing points of

Betty Jean Thiebaud and Book (detail, pl. 25), 1965–1969

Fig. 23. Richard Diebenkorn (American, 1922–1993), *Cityscape #3*, 1963. Oil on canvas, 47 x 50¼ in. Collection of Donald and Barbara Zucker. Courtesy of the Richard Diebenkorn Foundation

Surrealism are also at work, as are, once again, the roguish landscapes of *Krazy Kat* cartoons. Folk art even plays a role, especially, Thiebaud explains, in the way a folk artist might "shoot a street straight up into the air."[105] More than any of these, however, it was Diebenkorn's Berkeley cityscapes that Thiebaud credits as the single greatest influence (fig. 23).[106]

What proved most impactful about Diebenkorn's example was his manipulation of space and perspective. Whereas Diebenkorn made his scenes artful through abstraction, brushwork, and color, Thiebaud relied more on imagery. By manipulating perspective and scale, deemphasizing some sections and inflating the importance of others, and combining three-dimensional and flat passages, Thiebaud creates scenes that are blatantly unreal, even surreal, in scope and combination. And yet, at the same time, these scenes just manage to retain a sense of believability. Thiebaud states, "That dialogue between what was actually there and what was made up became the basis of the entire series."[107]

Many of these same qualities are also exemplified in the artist's Sacramento–San Joaquin Delta scenes, a group of paintings he started in the mid-1990s and unveiled in a show held at San Francisco's Campbell-Thiebaud Gallery in the fall of 1997. Though representations of water, levees, cultivated farmland, buildings, and sometimes even tiny tractors are included in these tableaus, adding elements of believability, the paintings do not depict the landscape as it is seen but as it is felt—and in a way that Thiebaud thought would have the most impact.

By the time he started these paintings, Thiebaud had looked at this landscape—and lived with it—for more than fifty years. He also, for a time, owned a home (Rosebud Farm) on the Sacramento River, a locale rich with surrounding orchards and farmland that allowed him to experience the delta and its agricultural production firsthand. Inspiration for these paintings came out of Thiebaud driving around and looking, and from his interest in the river as the lifeblood—"like the Nile Valley"—of California agriculture.[108] Childhood memories of the varied crop patterns and orchards of Southern California and his grandfather's farm there, and of growing fruits and vegetables on his family's ranch in Utah, factored in as well.[109]

As with his processed foods and built environments, Thiebaud's delta scenes evidence humanity's need to manipulate. Just as his pies and cakes were made by bakers, and his city scenes by architects and builders, Thiebaud's river and delta lands have been heavily modified by levees, buildings, and farming. He then further processes the landscape through his memory and intellect to create reality-based fantasies not only of the landscape itself, but of the human activity that has shaped it. "I'm not just interested in the pictorial aspects of the landscape," he explains, "see a pretty place and try to paint it—but in some way to manage it,

manipulate it, or see what I can turn it into."[110] Although the delta landscape he portrays is flat, he does not typically portray it as such, instead standing it on end to create a sweeping and expansive view. Within this space, he limns subsections through various perspectives and vantage points, the whole reading as a bird's-eye perspective that is, in reality, much more complicated. Some of this approach comes out of the discoveries he made when looking at Chinese paintings at the Metropolitan Museum of Art in New York, which coincided with the beginnings of his delta series. The use of space in Indian miniature paintings came into play as well, these also informing his color palette. The chromatically brilliant paintings of the French Fauves also contributed, as did Diebenkorn's landscapes and Ocean Park paintings. Nothing was off limits, as he sought to capture and communicate a deeply personal spirit of place:

> I tried to steal every kind of idea—Western, Eastern—and the use of everything I could think of—atmospheric perspective, size differences, color differences, overlapping, exaggeration, linear perspective, planar and sequential recessions—and to do that with the kind of vision I talked about before with as many ways of seeing, in the same picture— clear focus, hazy, squinting, glancing, staring, and even sort of inner seeing, a blind inner seeing as in day dreams or dreaming when the eyes are closed and not seeing anything but what you see inwardly.[111]

Thiebaud continues to paint landscapes like these even now, though he has also made a return to beach subjects, a series prompted by his family's purchase of a condominium in Laguna Beach, California, in 2002. Ever responsive to his environment, Thiebaud was compelled enough by what he could see from his beach overlook to want to depict it. The works that resulted, like the rest of his paintings, were a combination of real and unreal—the coast, buildings, and beachgoers the products of observation captured in drawings, which when assembled and combined with personal memories, art-historical knowledge, and imagination, became works of art. Though new in conception, these paintings were also a return to the past, both to his childhood in Long Beach and to the coastal subjects he portrayed at that pivotal, turn-of-the-1960s moment when he began to find his voice.

The cliff and mountain paintings that followed were no different. Thiebaud's youthful proximity to sublime rock formations like Checkerboard Mesa and the Great Arch of Utah's Zion National Park certainly informed the cliffs and steep terrain he would paint now, as did California's Sierra scenery and the grandeur of Yosemite. When he held a show of these works in 2013 at the Paul Thiebaud Gallery (formerly Campbell-Thiebaud Gallery) in San Francisco, it was appropriately subtitled *Memory Mountains*. As the title implies, these portrayals are never literal, but extrapolations and interpretations—even caricatures—of the land, both the forms and colors being subjective. Thiebaud explained his motivation, "Presently I'm trying to combine mountains I have seen with what I would like to see."[112] The paintings were also experimental, as the strata of rock monuments were sometimes built up in literal relief with acrylic modeling paste and layers of ridged impasto to enhance their rocklike appearance.

Most recently, with another decade ending and the artist on the precipice of his one hundredth birthday, Thiebaud has returned to the figure, this time to circus performers, most of them clowns. These paintings deliberately undermine a current art-world taboo against such portrayals, which in the realm of the American circus

Fig. 24. *Clown and Makeup*, 2016. Oil on canvas, 24 x 30 in. Courtesy of the artist

(as opposed to art-historical portrayals of European harlequins or Pierrot of the commedia dell'arte), only a handful of artists have circumvented with success. Thiebaud has painted an occasional clown before but not in a focused series as now. Once again, caricature is critical to this pursuit, only it has become literal. This is, in many ways, a culmination of what Thiebaud has been doing all along: caricaturing what he sees. The paintings also evidence his longtime interest in the idea of object transference; paint is like clown makeup, and clown makeup is like paint (fig. 24). Furthermore, face paint creates the caricature just as the artist himself renders the caricature, a layering upon layering of meaning that makes perfect sense within Thiebaud's oeuvre—and perhaps only in Thiebaud's oeuvre. There is also, in this series, Thiebaud's familiar combination of nostalgia and optimism, loneliness and isolation. Although some clowns are buoyant with joy, others do not revel in their careers under the big top. They do, however, metaphorically suggest the life of a weary performer—perhaps the artist himself—who has spent a good deal of time beguiling crowds under a spotlight. ▲▼▲

NOTES

1. Wayne Thiebaud, quoted in Elaine O'Brien, "Locating Thiebaud," in *Wayne Thiebaud: Works from 1955 to 2003* (Sacramento, CA: University Library Gallery, California State University, Sacramento, 2003), 61.

2. Wayne Thiebaud, oral history interview by Susan Larsen, Archives of American Art, Smithsonian Institution, May 17–18, 2001.

3. Wayne Thiebaud, quoted in Victoria Dalkey, "Wayne Thiebaud's Rural Landscapes," in *Wayne Thiebaud: Landscapes* (San Francisco: Campbell-Thiebaud Gallery, 1997).

4. Thiebaud, interview by Larsen, Smithsonian.

5. Wayne Thiebaud, quoted in Hearne Pardee, "Wayne Thiebaud with Hearne Pardee," *Brooklyn Rail* (March 2019).

6. Laura Cumming, "A Perfect World," in *Wayne Thiebaud*, by Suzanne Swarts et al. (Wassenaar, Netherlands: Voorlinden, 2018), 58.

7. Wayne Thiebaud, quoted in John Arthur, *Realists at Work* (New York: Watson-Guptill, 1983), 120.

8. Gene Cooper, "Thiebaud, Theatre, and Extremism," in *Wayne Thiebaud: Survey 1947–1976*, by Gene Cooper et al. (Phoenix, AZ: Phoenix Art Museum, 1976), 13.

9. Thiebaud, quoted in Arthur, *Realists at Work*, 116.

10. Thiebaud, interview by Larsen, Smithsonian.

11. Thiebaud, interview by Larsen, Smithsonian.

12. Thiebaud, interview by Larsen, Smithsonian.

13. Thiebaud, interview by Larsen, Smithsonian.

14. Karen Tsujimoto, *Wayne Thiebaud* (San Francisco: San Francisco Museum of Modern Art, 1985), 20–21.

15. Thiebaud, interview by Larsen, Smithsonian.

16. One work was an oil titled *Grandpère*; the other was a watercolor called *Put to Pasture*.

17. Wayne Thiebaud, quoted in Mark Strand, ed., *Art of the Real: Nine American Figurative Painters* (New York: Clarkson N. Potter, 1983), 181.

18. Thiebaud, interview by Larsen, Smithsonian.

19. Tsujimoto, *Wayne Thiebaud*, 22.

20. Thiebaud, quoted in Tsujimoto, *Wayne Thiebaud*, 22.

21. O'Brien, "Locating Thiebaud," 64.

22. For a discussion of the influence of art history on Thiebaud's thinking, see Pardee, "Wayne Thiebaud with Hearne Pardee."

23. John C. Oglesby, "Ever Wonder What Artists Are Up To? Exhibit Tells You," *Sacramento (CA) Bee*, February 10, 1951.

24. W. C. G., "Painter, Sculptor Talk about Contemporary Art," *Sacramento (CA) Bee*, February 5, 1951.

25. "Assistant is Appointed for Crocker Gallery," *Sacramento (CA) Bee*, January 9, 1951.

26. Cooper, "Thiebaud, Theatre, and Extremism," 28.

27. In 1998, the institution accorded him an honorary doctor of fine arts degree.

28. As Thiebaud described, "Cubism in Six Minutes." Cooper, "Thiebaud, Theatre, and Extremism," 20.

29. Foster served as the model for Thiebaud's 1959 painting *Zither Player* (pl. 3), O'Brien, "Locating Thiebaud," 65.

30. He would for a short time even teach printmaking at the California School of Fine Arts (now the San Francisco Art Institute), filling in for Bay Area Figurative painter Nathan Oliveira. Arielle Hardy, "Chronology," in *Wayne Thiebaud: 1958–1968*, by Rachel Teagle et al. (Oakland, CA: University of California Press, 2018).

31. Wayne Thiebaud, quoted in Stephen C. McGough, *Thiebaud Selects Thiebaud: A Forty-Year Survey from Private Collections* (Sacramento, CA: Crocker Art Museum, 1996), 9–10.

32. Thiebaud, quoted in McGough, *Thiebaud Selects Thiebaud*, 10.

33. Thiebaud, interview by Larsen, Smithsonian. See also Adam Gopnik, "An American Painter," in *Wayne Thiebaud: A Paintings Retrospective*, by Steven A. Nash and Adam Gopnik (San Francisco: Fine Arts Museums of San Francisco, 2000), 48.

34. Wayne Thiebaud, quoted in Crocker Art Museum, "Wayne Thiebaud Paintings on Exhibit at Crocker Art Gallery," press release, 1957, exhibition files.

35. In addition to Bischoff, Diebenkorn, and Park, the artists included Joseph Brooks, William Theophilus Brown, Robert Downs, Bruce McGaw, Robert Qualters, Walter Snelgrove, Henry Villierme, James Weeks, and Paul Wonner.

36. Richard Diebenkorn, quoted in Paul Mills, *Contemporary Bay Area Figurative Painting* (Oakland, CA: Oakland Art Museum, 1957), 12.

37. These included artists Patrick Dullanty, Eben Jordan Haskell, Gregory Kondos, Jack Ogden, and Mel Ramos, as well as entrepreneur Russ Solomon. Haskell is the man depicted in Thiebaud's *Swimsuit Figures*, 1966.

38. The scenes are broken into four panels, with two flanking the entrance and one on each adjoining side of the building. The mural was recently cleaned and restored as part of a 2018–2019 renovation and rehabilitation of the building, which was added to the National Register of Historic Places in 2010.

39. Karen Tsujimoto states that Thiebaud had been influenced by Arthur Upham Pope's essays on Persian art. Tsujimoto, *Wayne Thiebaud*, 26.

40. Thiebaud was elevated to associate professor in 1963 and full professor in 1967. He became professor emeritus in 1990.

41. *Painters at UC Davis* (Davis, CA: Richard L. Nelson Gallery, University of California, Davis, 1984), 8.

42. Thiebaud, interview by Larsen, Smithsonian.

43. Ralph Johnson, quoted in *Painters at UC Davis*, 8.

44. These included Gilhooly, who started out as a student, Richard Notkin, Richard Shaw, Peter VandenBerge, the painter/ceramist Maija Zack (later Peeples-Bright), and others.

45. Wayne Thiebaud, quoted in Isabelle Dervaux, *Wayne Thiebaud: Draftsman* (New York: Morgan Library and Museum, 2018), 149.

46. Invitation reproduced in Teagle et al., *Wayne Thiebaud*, 73.

47. Thiebaud, quoted in McGough, *Thiebaud Selects Thiebaud*, 10.

48. Thiebaud, quoted in Dervaux, *Draftsman*, 149–150.

49. Wayne Thiebaud, quoted in Thomas Albright, "Wayne Thiebaud: Scrambling Around with Ordinary Problems," *Art News* 77, no. 2 (February 1978): 86.

50. Paul Cézanne, letter to Emile Bernard, April 15, 1904, quoted in Erle Loran, *Cézanne's Composition: Analysis of His Form with Diagrams and Photographs of His Motifs*, 3d ed. (Berkeley, CA: University of California Press, 1970), 9.

51. Gopnik, "An American Painter," 50.

52. Wayne Thiebaud, quoted in Richard Wollheim, "On Thiebaud and

Diebenkorn: Richard Wollheim Talks to Wayne Thiebaud," in *California Landscapes: Richard Diebenkorn / Wayne Thiebaud* (New York: Acquavella Galleries, 2018), 65.

53. Wayne Thiebaud, quoted in Jori Finkel, "Wayne Thiebaud Examines a Still Life," *Los Angeles Times*, June 30, 2013.

54. Thiebaud, quoted in McGough, *Thiebaud Selects Thiebaud*, 9.

55. Thiebaud, quoted in McGough, *Thiebaud Selects Thiebaud*, 9.

56. Wayne Thiebaud, quoted in Eve Aschheim and Chris Daubert, *Episodes with Wayne Thiebaud: Four Interviews 2009–2011* (New York: Black Square Editions, 2014), 9.

57. Thiebaud, quoted in Aschheim and Daubert, *Episodes*, 9.

58. Thiebaud, quoted in Gopnik, "An American Painter," 55.

59. Thiebaud, quoted in O'Brien, "Locating Thiebaud," 64.

60. Thiebaud, quoted in Wollheim, "On Thiebaud and Diebenkorn," 64.

61. Wayne Thiebaud, "Is a Lollipop Tree Worth Painting?" *San Francisco Sunday Chronicle*, July 15, 1962.

62. John Coplans, *Wayne Thiebaud* (Pasadena, CA: Pasadena Art Museum, 1968), 28.

63. Thiebaud, quoted in Strand, *Art of the Real*, 189.

64. Thiebaud, "Lollipop Tree?"

65. Thiebaud, "Lollipop Tree?"

66. Thiebaud, interview by Larsen, Smithsonian.

67. Thiebaud, interview by Larsen, Smithsonian.

68. "Art: The Slice-of-Cake School," *Time* 79, no. 19 (May 11, 1962): 52.

69. The Museum of Modern Art purchased *Cut Meringues* (1961); the Wadsworth Atheneum acquired *Half Cakes* (1961).

70. Clement Greenberg, "America Takes the Lead, 1945–1965," in *Clement Greenberg: The Collected Essays and Criticism*, vol. 4, *Modernism with a Vengeance, 1957–1969*, ed. John O'Brian (Chicago: University of Chicago Press, 1993), 215.

71. Max Kozloff, "Art," *The Nation*, May 5, 1962, 406.

72. Thomas B. Hess, "Wayne Thiebaud," *Art News* 61, no. 3 (May 1962): 17.

73. Donald Judd, "In the Galleries," *Arts Magazine* 36, no. 10 (September 1962): 49.

74. Thiebaud, "Lollipop Tree?"

75. Clement Greenberg, "After Abstract Expressionism," in *Clement Greenberg: The Collected Essays and Criticism*, vol. 4, *Modernism with a Vengeance, 1957–1969*, ed. John O'Brian (Chicago: University of Chicago Press, 1993), 134.

76. "Slice-of-Cake School," 52.

77. Thiebaud, quoted in Aschheim and Daubert, *Episodes*, 25.

78. Wayne Thiebaud, quoted in Gene Cooper, "Wayne Thiebaud: Beach Memories," in *Thiebaud: Seventy Years of Painting* (Sacramento, CA: LeBaron's Fine Art, 2007), 14.

79. Judd, "In the Galleries," 48.

80. Brian O'Doherty, "Art: America Seen Through Stomach," *New York Times*, April 28, 1962.

81. Pepe Karmel, "The Lonely Crowd: Men and Women in the Art of Wayne Thiebaud" in John Wilmerding, *Wayne Thiebaud* (New York: Acquavella Galleries, 2012), 34.

82. Wayne Thiebaud, quoted in "Looking through Wayne's Eyes," in *Wayne Thiebaud*, by Suzanne Swarts et al. (Wassenaar, Netherlands: Voorlinden, 2018), 113.

83. Thiebaud, "Lollipop Tree?"

84. Allan Stone, quoted in Tsujimoto, *Wayne Thiebaud*, 36-37.

85. Thiebaud, quoted in Arthur, *Realists at Work*, 120.

86. Wayne Thiebaud, quoted in Michael Zakian, "Wayne Thiebaud and the Folk Art Ideal," in *Wayne Thiebaud: Works from 1955 to 2003* (Sacramento, CA: University Library Gallery, California State University, Sacramento, 2003), 13.

87. Adam Gopnik, "The Art World: Window Gazing," *New Yorker*, April 29, 1991, 79.

88. Jack Kerouac, *On the Road* (New York: Viking Press, 1955), 48.

89. Wayne Thiebaud, quoted in Gopnik, "The Art World: Window Gazing," 79.

90. Wayne Thiebaud, quoted in A. Le Grace G. Benson and David H. R. Shearer, "An Interview with Wayne Thiebaud," *Leonardo* 2, no. 1 (January 1969): 70.

91. Thiebaud, "Lollipop Tree?"

92. Thiebaud, "Lollipop Tree?"

93. Wayne Thiebaud, quoted in Susan Stowens, "Wayne Thiebaud: Beyond Pop Art," *American Artist* 44, no. 458 (September 1980): 102.

94. Rachel Teagle, "Presence from Absence: Wayne Thiebaud and the Future of Painting," in *Wayne Thiebaud: 1958–1968*, by Rachel Teagle et al. (Oakland, CA: University of California Press, 2018), 153.

95. Wayne Thiebaud, quoted in Dan Tooker, "Wayne Thiebaud," *Art International* 18, no. 9 (November 1974): 22.

96. Thiebaud, quoted in Cooper, "Beach Memories," 11.

97. Betty Jean Thiebaud, quoted in Teagle, "Presence from Absence," 38.

98. Thiebaud, quoted in Benson and Shearer, "An Interview with Wayne Thiebaud," 66.

99. Thiebaud, quoted in Tooker, "Wayne Thiebaud," 22.

100. Wayne Thiebaud, quoted in Gail Gordon, "Thiebaud Puts a Visual Feast on Canvas," *California Aggie* (Davis, CA), February 9, 1983.

101. Wayne Thiebaud, quoted in Pardee, "Wayne Thiebaud with Hearne Pardee;" Wayne Thiebaud, quoted in Aschheim and Daubert, *Episodes*, 45.

102. Wayne Thiebaud, foreword to *Drawn to Excellence: Masters of Cartoon Art* (San Francisco: Cartoon Art Museum, 1988).

103. Wayne Thiebaud, quoted in Richard Wollheim, "An Interview with Wayne Thiebaud," in *Wayne Thiebaud: Cityscapes* (San Francisco: Campbell-Thiebaud Gallery, 1993).

104. Wayne Thiebaud, quoted in Steven A. Nash "Unbalancing Acts: Wayne Thiebaud Reconsidered," in *Wayne Thiebaud: A Paintings Retrospective*, by Steven A. Nash and Adam Gopnik (San Francisco: Fine Arts Museums of San Francisco, 2000), 31.

105. Thiebaud, quoted in Albright, "Scrambling Around," 86; see also Tsujimoto, *Wayne Thiebaud*, 131.

106. Wollheim, "On Thiebaud and Diebenkorn," 67.

107. Thiebaud, quoted in Wollheim, "An Interview with Wayne Thiebaud."

108. Thiebaud, quoted in McGough, *Thiebaud Selects Thiebaud*, 12.

109. Nash, "Unbalancing Acts," 33.

110. Thiebaud, quoted in Gordon, "Visual Feast," 2.

111. Thiebaud, quoted in Dalkey, "Wayne Thiebaud's Rural Landscapes."

112. Thiebaud, quoted in Aschheim and Daubert, *Episodes*, 84.

2

CONFECTIONS AND
CANDIED LANDSCAPES

Margaretta Markle Lovell

Through the alchemy of art, Wayne Thiebaud's subjects operate on our appetites, foster a deep sense of longing, and allude quietly to moments of pathos. Whether roadways, portraits, or breakfast—they tend to be approached frontally, offering up their identities with the frank immediacy and trusting openness of deep friendship. Above all, his works function as invitations, beckoning the viewer and alluding, through the powerful sense of vision, to other senses: touch, taste, smell, sometimes sound, and, almost always, memory. As one appreciative critic of Thiebaud has observed, "There is about the work the same kind of straightforwardness there is about the man."[1] His subjects are, however, almost never as straightforward as they appear.

In considering Thiebaud's investigations of America's foodways and the built environment, a good place to begin is with a work that contains both. *Cherry Stand* (1964; pl. 12) is one of several early works that record and comment on informal food sites—roadside stands and beachfront shacks that announce through their pictorial and verbal signage such delights as "CHERRIES" and "ICE COLD" watermelon. The signage in this small but characteristic work—a proffered watermelon slice nearly as large as the shack—shouts welcome over a bounty of smaller fruits in overflowing baskets and bins gathered under an overhanging roof. Sheltered here from the hot summer sun casting sharp shadows, we are promised sweetness, shade, and abundance, or, as Thiebaud put it, "a kind of metaphor of plentitude."[2] The elements of this early etching—food treats, vernacular landscapes, and the effects of intense light on forms of all kinds, remain hallmarks of Thiebaud's work for the ensuing prolific decades. The watermelon gets complicated with a knife, and the landscapes get complicated

Strawberry Cone (detail, pl. 31), 1969

with the loss of the horizon, but key elements of the America Thiebaud tells us he loves—and wants us to really see and think about—are here already in 1964.[3] Similarly, the America he eschews—the branded, boxed, and canned foods of Warhol fame, and the grandiose gestures of Bierstadt's Yosemite, are absent, and they will remain absent in the years to come.

National Foods and Foodways

Evoking the lowbrow haunts, practices, and celebratory foodways of our common national culture, Thiebaud's subjects—in a wide variety of media—teach us to think about the sites, activities, and actors in our overlooked stalwart and festive everyday food-service world. *Bacon and Eggs* (pl. 13), a 1964 etching, summons us as hungry viewers to a diner breakfast—two sunny-side-up eggs, slices of bacon, two pieces of commercial white-bread toast with two equally square pats of butter, a portion of jam, a glass of water, and a cup of joe. The image is both particular—one meal, one eater, one event—and universal. We quickly amplify the picture and build in our minds the clatter of heavy restaurant-ware on Formica, a spatula-wielding short-order cook at the grill in the back, an efficient waitress with a green order pad moving between the kitchen and brightly lit booths. There are other ways to breakfast in this country, but this one is familiar to us all.

Sometimes, in a deft metonymic mode, Thiebaud conjures that place, those workers, and those foods in still-life works of just the service items on hand at every table—the sugar dispenser with its little hinged port, the squat napkin dispenser, and a matched pair of salt and pepper shakers. We know where we are, what the plastic-sleeved menu will feel like, what foods it will offer, what tastes we will experience in the presence of this particular set of objects. Thiebaud comes to this site not as an urban voyeur but as a former employee of such places, and as a painter whose early exhibition venues included the snack bar of Sacramento's Starlite Drive-In.[4] Later, the same sense of spatial and cultural recognition will be triggered by a single item. *Salt Shaker* (1979; pl. 40), for instance, portrays the heavy glass, metal-capped shaker with its sturdy hexagonal form—an object that we will not see in white-tablecloth restaurants. But, we will see it anywhere in an American diner, truck stop, or livery-street café, where blue-collar workers pause for table or counter service in the middle of a long workday. As Thiebaud has observed, "I think the big difference in America as compared to Europe is that the food here is the same wherever you go, even down to the napkins and the salt and pepper shakers on the restaurant tables."[5]

On one occasion, Thiebaud alludes so obliquely to lunching in a diner that only insiders will get it. *Window View* (1971/1981; pl. 33) depicts the Marin Headlands from the corner table in Louis', a small cash-only diner with communal tables perched on a San Francisco cliff overlooking the Pacific. Louis' affords a view of the heavily laden, transpacific freighters approaching the Golden Gate, and, across the water, the steep headlands of Marin County. This view, then, is not just an early venture by Thiebaud into a genre that will become increasingly important to him—landscape—it is a painting redolent of the (unpictured) lunch fare of such eateries: hamburgers, hot dogs, french fries, grilled-cheese, and tuna-melt sandwiches to be followed, of course, by pie a la mode or a sundae in a heavy glass dish.

Better known than the diner images (its foods, its table setups, and its views), are other sites of blue-collar respite from work: the bakery, the delicatessen, the cafeteria, and the ice-cream parlor. Works picturing these places and their familiar food presentations remain central to our understanding of Thiebaud's pictorial analysis of the world. *Bakery Counter* (1993; pl. 73),

Food Bowls (1992/2000/2005; pl. 72), and *Untitled (Deli)* (2016; pl. 95) depict confections and ready-to-eat deli foods within a kind of gustatory proscenium. Cakes, cookies, salads, and cheeses tilt toward us in their theatrical presentation cases, and we, their obliging audience, attend closely to the cookery-craftsmanship that they represent. Above all, these images speak to the amplitude and variety of professionally prepared treats available virtually everywhere in this country, or, in Thiebaud's terms, "a celebration of very ordinary commonplace things."[6] Yet, they are also painterly problems in geometry: "I took three basic shapes to work with: a rectangle, an ellipse or a circle and a triangle. Well, that's a piece of pie."[7]

Especially expressive of the status and amplitude of sweets in mid-twentieth-century American culture, the cafeteria-presentation of pies in their orderly, almost military lineups reminds us of the difficulty of making choices in such a world. These arrays position us as customers sliding sturdy cafeteria trays, already laden, along the line. This is the eater's view of pie, which, as every child knows, must be eaten from the point toward the crust. Thiebaud's pie portions are not just familiar as simulated taste treats, they are art-school exercises in the depiction of geometric volumes, recession, and the active character of shadows. In speaking about such works, Thiebaud tends to shy away from inquiries that probe the possibility of symbolism or social commentary, emphasizing instead the formal, painterly problems of depiction and vision. "I tend to view the subject matter without trying to be too opaque with respect to its symbolic reference," he offers. "For instance, pie offers a great combination of problems, like a meringue pie both absorbs and reflects light . . . combined with the geometric clarity of its very basic shape."[8]

Among his most tempting confections are ice-cream cones—backlit, standing at attention, and enjoying a solo spotlight. Thiebaud tells us that he paints food from memory, as well as from direct study, but we cannot help but feel a note of anxiety about these time-sensitive meltables posing for their portraits, especially when we learn that he sometimes creates his remarkable light effects under "very strong light bulbs in my studio, a daylight bulb, a 3200° Kelvin photoflood light, which illuminates a subject, in some ways, like the sun."[9] The "edge effect" in images like *Three Ice Cream Cones* (1964/1986; fig. 29, p. 70) solves the painterly problem of how one can make "the painting . . . create its own light, . . . create its own energizing forces."[10] These are not, in other words, transcriptions of vision but crafted projects undertaken to simulate experience, activate memory, and work as independent objects of aesthetic interest. Thiebaud's recurrent interest in ice cream may reflect, in part, not only the appropriateness of rhyming its frozen substance with impasto passages of paint but also the rich variety of bright colors in which ice cream is made. Ice cream provides him an occasion to think about color as something arbitrary, playful, and intensely important: "If you are working from memory you have a much wider way of orchestrating potential variations."[11] We also see this central focus on color in such works as *Pastel Scatter* (1972; pl. 35), which studies the tools of art through an open box of pastels, not tidy in rainbow sequence but scattered in seemingly random groups of chromatic juxtaposition. The pastelist, the painter, and the ice-cream maker have in common an enormous array of color choices and effects, a fact that Thiebaud exploits.

The bright red candied apples of fall, a confection that comes in only one signature color, are a subject Thiebaud returns to decade after decade in various media. The apples, encased in a vermillion sugar jacket that pools as it hardens into a kind of platform, rest with their sticks in the air in regimental groups of three, six, or nine (pls. 30, 51, 81).

The motif exhibits variety in the sticks, which lean at slightly different angles, but the overall effect is one of sameness and repetition rather than sameness with variation, which we more often see thematized in Thiebaud's work. In a rare conjunction of human and edible subjects, we find these apples as a bright water-color vignette on a sheet that, in a startling visual non sequitur, also contains two pen-and-ink profiles of influential critic Clement Greenberg (pl. 51). Greenberg was a regular at the New York club where, in Thiebaud's 1956–1957 year in that city, the artist spent Friday evenings with other luminaries of the New York School, including Willem de Kooning, Harold Rosenberg, and Barnett Newman, engaging in "all kind of arguing and talking."[12] Greenberg—a formalist who championed Abstract Expressionism and had severe words for representational art—would not have been sympathetic to seeing his portrait paired with candied treats. Perhaps the conjunction of these disparate elements on a single sheet is not deliberately meaningful; or, perhaps, it is one of Thiebaud's own "really interesting puzzles" that obliquely memorializes, thirty years later, the periodic sociable assembly of a group of men (apples) intensely interested in art during an urban sojourn that Thiebaud speaks of in the most positive terms.[13] And yet, he left New York and the New York School to establish himself on very different terms far away.

From 1940, Greenberg had been explaining and boosting contemporary New York–based artists to collectors, artists, gallerists, and the public. From the pages of the *Partisan Review*, the *Nation*, *Art Digest*, and the *New York Times*, Greenberg valorized a less-is-more aesthetic in the work of Barnett Newman, Mark Rothko, and Clyfford Still. Of these, he was particularly taken by "the simple and firm sensuousness and the splendor, of Rothko's pictures."[14] He described the process of "discarding" the "expendable conventions" of painting as "self-purification," a process in which art is increasingly a matter of geometry, color, abstraction, flatness, simplification, and emptiness, a matter of "relations of color, shape and line largely divorced from descriptive connotations."[15] The nouns that Greenberg associated with the work of the artists he endorsed include *honesty*, *integrity*, *probity*, *authenticity*, *truth*, *intensity*, *power*, *boldness*, *freedom*, and *independence*.[16] Among the critiques that he flung at artists outside his charmed circle of "genuine" practitioners of Abstract Expressionism, one finds *provincial*, *insecure*, *feeble*, *awkward*, and *inconsequential*, judgments intended to clarify the preeminence of the "strong and original talents" of the artists Greenberg endorsed.[17]

While it is clear that Thiebaud agreed with the formal principles of geometry, color, and simplicity that Greenberg exalted in his extended manifesto, it is also clear that he has never discarded "descriptive connotations," nor endorsed the hierarchical heroes-and-goats value judgments that Greenberg relished. Indeed, we see a gentle reproof to Greenberg's posturing in Thiebaud's remark, "Critics seem to go out of their minds with the most wild jargon about what art is. I agree with them that art is going to save the world. But it is not going to save it with heroic gestures but with nuances of fact."[18]

Candied apples also appear in this catalogue as an undated, untitled drawing that includes four variations on the theme, all enclosed in neat rectangles—hovering like memories—above three chunks of watermelon, one stuck with a fork, one poniarded with a knife, and a third, prone (pl. 44). The watermelon with knife comes front-and-center in a work of its own in 1989 (pl. 63). "Ambiguity," Thiebaud has remarked, "is as important as specificity."[19]

Pastel Scatter (detail, pl. 35), 1972

Fig. 25. *Wayne Thiebaud with artist Elaine de Kooning at her New York studio*, 1960s. Photograph by Betty Jean Thiebaud

Local Landscapes

During the 1970s and '80s Thiebaud turned increasingly to landscapes, but unlike the steady ground line in *Cherry Stand* (1964; pl. 12), which bisects the image, the horizon in depictions of San Francisco—and later of the Sacramento–San Joaquin Delta—becomes an unsettled and unsettling element.[20] Having bought and rehabbed a small house in a working-class neighborhood on Potrero Hill in 1972, the painter found himself living in a topographically eccentric place that piqued his curiosity, where he could go out into the city or "paint out of my back window."[21] *Untitled (City View)* (1993; pl. 77) suggests this conjunction of domesticity, observation, and investigation. Notoriously steep, the streets of San Francisco became the focus of

Thiebaud's attention, and he used their vertiginous trajectories and intersections in an investigation of what is, to most Californians and strangers alike, an unfamiliar, disorienting, and somewhat surreal built environment.

Seemingly frank, frontal, and documentary, such works as *Street and Shadow* of 1982–1983 and reworked in 1996 (pl. 43) are cityscapes, but ones in which the buildings have less of a role than the asphalt roadways. Streets and their underlying topography are the primary, runaway-crazy actors in these little dramas about space and place. Always generous with his sources, Thiebaud credits his interest in streetscapes to his friend Richard Diebenkorn: "The street pictures . . . came out of Dick's Berkeley series and his street scenes. . . . One of the things that Dick uses a great deal is a kind of X."[22] In *Street and Shadow* we see this X dramatized in a wobbly intersection. Thiebaud describes the visceral effect of these streetscapes:

> I was first fascinated by those plunging streets, where you get down to an intersection and all four streets take off in different directions and positions. There was a sense of displacement, or indeterminate fixed positional stability. That led me to this sense of 'verticality' that you get in San Francisco. You look at a hill, and visually, it doesn't look as if the cars would be able to stay on it and grip. It's a very precarious state of tension, like a tightrope walk.[23]

Thiebaud reports that other influential aspects of Diebenkorn's street scenes include "cascading roads coming down, with shadows being cast. And I frankly used that device and made it steeper and a little more parallel to the picture plane, in order to see if I could establish some sort of energetic geometry, which would make it as much abstract as realistic."[24] For most viewers, what is abstract—pattern, form, color relationships—is what we can see in the painting across the room. What is realistic, or at least referential to the world we inhabit, with recognizable objects like buildings and forces like gravity, is what one can see upon closer approach.

While critics have opined that Thiebaud's "cityscapes unmistakably belong to a car-bound, gas-driven, contemporary America . . . a commuter's view," in most of these views no vehicles negotiate the streets—the car being only a potential actor in the pantomime.[25] Thiebaud suggests that we imagine negotiating these roadways. We respond to these roller-coaster street scenes somatically—with something like disorientation, anxiety, or fear—just as we respond to the food images viscerally, with recognition, memory, and desire.

Much of Thiebaud's interest in landscape has less to do with nature than with the ways humans have managed, manipulated, and mapped their concerns onto natural environments. As he has put it, "[I have a] fascination with landscape . . . as something that is made, not made, unmade, changed, ongoing."[26] San Francisco offers one extreme case of an "ongoing" landscape. Even more chameleonlike are the river-fed farmlands of the Sacramento–San Joaquin Delta, where, in the 1990s, Thiebaud bought and fixed up what he described as "a big old dilapidated mansion . . . in the middle of pear orchards, and the river was right in front of the house."[27] Here, amidst rich agricultural lands protected by levees and laced by a maze of waterways, he began to produce an extraordinary group of paintings focused, as described by his friend, philosopher Richard Wollheim, on "the great oozing majesty of the river, with its variety of channels, and the adjacent harlequinade of water meadow, plow, orchard, pasture, lines of poplars, and fields put to some unidentifiable agro-industrial use . . . a patchwork of fields, each patch lying in some provocative disharmony with its neighbor."[28] This is not a part of California known to tourists; indeed, most Californians have never paused there. But in Thiebaud's hands it becomes as notable and stunning as the well-known, well-traveled beauties of Napa or Tahoe. What is made most clear is that this is a well-husbanded, dynamic place, a place where water and sunshine and human effort combine to create livelihoods for many—and food for millions. As with the truck-stop salt cellar, what Thiebaud is teaching us is that "commonplace objects [and landscapes are] . . . intrinsically elegant, beautiful. . . . They are icons."[29]

Thiebaud draws on a combination of perception and memory to create paintings that bring common objects and common experiences to our attention in ways we had not imagined. Bringing to bear a lifetime

Fig. 26. *Wayne Thiebaud in his office at the University of California, Davis*, n.d. Photographer unknown

of experimentation and experience, he constructs works that, in his words, create their own light.[30] But that is not the end of it. The viewer also brings recognition, memory, and responsive feelings to the image. There are no solo ventures in art, Thiebaud would say, the art object "doesn't come from an individual. It's communal."[31] It exists in a communication not just between painter and audience but also between artists working, looking, and talking together, as well as in the extended longitudinal trajectory of artists over time. Thiebaud haunts museums, reasoning that "I see the museum as a kind of bureau of standards setting criteria of excellence," the place where we can see, study, and learn from those who have engaged in this difficult life of artmaking throughout history.[32] And museums and exhibitions, of course, are the places where the rest of us can engage with—and learn from—samples of his life's work. Above all, what he teaches us is to see the ordinary as extraordinary and to recognize it as "evidence of what we are as people."[33] ▲▼▲

Untitled (City View) (detail, pl. 77), 1993

NOTES

1. Jan Butterfield, "Wayne Thiebaud: A Feast for the Senses," *Arts Magazine* 52, no. 2 (October 1977): 132.

2. Wayne Thiebaud, quoted in John Coplans, *Wayne Thiebaud* (Pasadena, CA: Pasadena Art Museum, 1968), 24.

3. Wayne Thiebaud, quoted in Alessia Masi, "Interview to Wayne Thiebaud," *Wayne Thiebaud at Museo Morandi* (Mantua, Italy: Corraini Edizioni, 2011).

4. Wayne Thiebaud, in Michael Kimmelman, "Wayne Thiebaud," in *Portraits: Talking with Artists at the Met, The Modern, the Louvre and Elsewhere* (New York: Random House, 1998), 160; Meredith Tromble, "A Conversation with Wayne Thiebaud," *Artweek* 29 (January 1998): 15.

5. Thiebaud, quoted in Coplans, *Wayne Thiebaud*, 23.

6. Wayne Thiebaud, quoted in A. Le Grace G. Benson, and David H. R. Shearer, "An Interview with Wayne Thiebaud," *Leonardo* 2, no. 1 (January 1969): 66.

7. Thiebaud, quoted in Benson and Shearer, "An Interview with Wayne Thiebaud," 66.

8. Wayne Thiebaud, quoted in Dan Tooker, "Wayne Thiebaud," *Art International* 18, no. 9 (November 1974): 22.

9. Thiebaud, quoted in Benson and Shearer, "An Interview with Wayne Thiebaud," 71.

10. Thiebaud, quoted in Coplans, *Wayne Thiebaud*, 32.

11. Thiebaud, quoted in Tromble, "A Conversation with Wayne Thiebaud," 15.

12. Wayne Thiebaud, oral history interview by Susan Larsen, Archives of American Art, Smithsonian Institution, May 17–18, 2001.

13. Thiebaud, quoted in Masi, "Interview to Wayne Thiebaud."

14. Clement Greenberg, "'American-Type' Painting," in *Art and Culture: Critical Essays* (Boston: Beacon Press, 1961), 226.

15. Greenberg, "'American-Type' Painting," 208; Clement Greenberg, "Abstract and Representational," in *Clement Greenberg: The Collected Essays and Criticism*, vol. 3, *Affirmations and Refusals, 1950–1956*, ed. John O'Brian (Chicago: University of Chicago Press, 1993), 191.

16. Clement Greenberg, "Abstract Art," in *Clement Greenberg: The Collected Essays and Criticism*, vol. 1, *Perceptions and Judgements, 1939–1944*, ed. John O'Brian (Chicago: University of Chicago Press, 1988), 203; Clement Greenberg, "'Feeling Is All,'" in *Clement Greenberg: The Collected Essays and Criticism*, vol. 3, *Affirmations and Refusals, 1950–1956*, ed. John O'Brian (Chicago: University of Chicago Press, 1993), 99, 100, 101, 104; Greenberg, "Abstract and Representational," 134; Greenberg, "'American-Type' Painting," 208, 217, 218, 225.

17. Clement Greenberg, "The Present Prospects of American Painting and Sculpture," in *Clement Greenberg: The Collected Essays and Criticism*, vol. 2, *Arrogant Purpose, 1945–1949*, ed. John O'Brian (Chicago: University of Chicago Press, 1988), 165; Clement Greenberg, "Our Period Style," in *Clement Greenberg: The Collected Essays and Criticism*, vol. 2, *Arrogant Purpose, 1945–1949*, ed. John O'Brian (Chicago: University of Chicago Press, 1988), 325; Clement Greenberg, "Some Advantages of Provincialism," in *Clement Greenberg: The Collected Essays and Criticism*, vol. 3, *Affirmations and Refusals, 1950–1956*, ed. John O'Brian (Chicago: University of Chicago Press, 1993), 162; Greenberg, "Abstract Art," 199; Greenberg, "'American-Type' Painting," 216, 228; Robert Rosenblum, "The Primal American Scene," in *The Natural Paradise: Painting in America 1800–1950*, ed. Kynaston McShine (New York: Museum of Modern Art, 1976), 15–18.

18. Thiebaud, quoted in Benson and Shearer, "An Interview with Wayne Thiebaud," 72.

19. Thiebaud, quoted in Kimmelman, "Wayne Thiebaud," 164.

20. Margaretta Markle Lovell, "City, River, Mountain: Wayne Thiebaud's California," *Panorama: Journal of the Association of Historians of American Art* 3, no. 2 (Fall 2017), https://doi.org/10.24926/24716839.1602.

21. Wayne Thiebaud, interview with the author, August 11, 2016; Steven A. Nash, "Unbalancing Acts: Wayne Thiebaud Reconsidered," in *Wayne Thiebaud: A Paintings Retrospective*, by Steven A. Nash and Adam Gopnik (San Francisco: Fine Arts Museums of San Francisco, 2000), 27.

22. Wayne Thiebaud, quoted in Richard Wollheim, "On Thiebaud and Diebenkorn: Richard Wollheim Talks to Wayne Thiebaud," *Modern Painters: A Quarterly Journal of the Fine Arts* 4, no. 3 (Autumn 1991): 66.

23. Wayne Thiebaud, quoted in Susan Stowens, "Wayne Thiebaud: Beyond Pop Art," *American Artist* 44, no. 458 (September 1980): 50.

24. Thiebaud, interview with the author, August 11, 2016.

25. Adam Gopnik, "An American Painter," in *Wayne Thiebaud: A Paintings Retrospective*, by Steven A. Nash and Adam Gopnik (San Francisco: Fine Arts Museums of San Francisco, 2000), 58.

26. Thiebaud, interview with the author, August 11, 2016.

27. Thiebaud, interview by Larsen, Smithsonian.

28. Richard Wollheim, "Wayne Thiebaud: Green River Lands," *Artforum* 38, no. 2 (October 1999): 135.

29. Thiebaud, quoted in Benson and Shearer, "An Interview with Wayne Thiebaud," 69–70.

30. Wollheim, "On Thiebaud and Diebenkorn," 64–65.

31. Thiebaud, quoted in Tromble, "A Conversation with Wayne Thiebaud," 15

32. Wayne Thiebaud, quoted in Rachael Blackburn, "Interview," *Wayne Thiebaud: Fifty Years of Painting* (Kansas City, MO: Kemper Museum of Contemporary Art, 2003), 2.

33. Thiebaud, quoted in Masi, "Interview to Wayne Thiebaud."

3

DRAWING AND EMPATHY: THIEBAUD ON PAPER

Hearne Pardee

In his 2000 lecture at the National Gallery of Art in Washington, DC, Wayne Thiebaud defended the "dead" art of painting—flat, silent, and static—by appealing to empathy: "our capacity to transfer our bodies into things outside ourselves." The intersubjective experience of empathy brings artworks to life and, without it, "we would not have a culture or civilization."[1] In Thiebaud's work, empathy involves not just emotional identification with a subject but also a tactile, bodily experience—"not so much mental as a mind/body complex."[2] It involves our relationship to forces ranging from the gravity in vertiginous cityscapes to the animation of inert materials in still lifes. For Thiebaud, this empathic, physical engagement operates across media and stylistic conventions and unites the varied works featured here. Also uniting them is the underlying practice of drawing, which transcends media. It is a medium of speculation and analysis that demands empathy through close observation of objects, as well as in terms of spatial orientation. Drawing's conceptual character also provides a chronological thread for Thiebaud that ties his tabletops to his mountaintops.

When art critic John Berger condemned painting for catering to the wealthy with seductive renderings of glamorous flesh and expensive fabrics, he made an exception for artist William Blake, who eschewed the sensual substantiality of oil paint in favor of drawing and mixed media.[3] While more committed than Blake to depicting an object's substance, Thiebaud often also translates images from one drawing medium to another and experiments with layers and combinations of materials, demonstrating a commitment to drawing as a tool of investigation that can stimulate the imagination. *Sardines* (1982/1990; pl. 45), for example, participates in a long tradition of using fish as a demonstration of virtuosity in painting, though here the medium is watercolor applied to a print. In it, liquid color flows over finely etched lines that evoke shimmering, silver fish scales and arouse an aesthetic frisson. *Lipsticks* (1988; pl. 59), on the other hand, uses dry, brittle lines in colored pencil to animate the bright striations on shiny, metallic cylinders. Unlike his oil renderings of meringue, frosting, and ice cream, which might be subject to Berger's critique (although they are hardly addressed to the wealthy), these layerings allow line, along with color's tactile, material immediacy to claim attention in its own right.

Early Training

Thiebaud's exceptional combination of relaxed experimentation and focused discipline extends back to his unconventional training. As an aspiring cartoonist and commercial artist, he learned the tricks of illustration—"clichés"—which could be called upon if an art director demanded quick results: "You have to figure out how to make all these different things: an apple, a pear, a pineapple."[4] At the same time, his mentors also

Park Place (detail, pl. 79), 1995

conveyed a deep respect for the accomplishments of the Old Masters. When Thiebaud visited New York City in 1956, marketing his cartoons while acquainting himself with the Abstract Expressionists, he especially admired Willem de Kooning, a skilled draftsman trained in Holland who shared Thiebaud's background in commercial art. Thiebaud was impressed by the "succinct reductiveness" of de Kooning's paintings, as well as by his use of the "shorthand of figure painting" in his gestural marks.[5] When de Kooning challenged him to discover what he really wanted to paint, Thiebaud responded by combining Abstract Expressionist paint handling with the geometric shapes and bold shading of graphic design—a "kind of drawing that comes out of caricature"—to generate his densely worked paintings of foods and utensils. "Caricature is a wonderful tool," Thiebaud explains. "What I am referring to is some measure of exaggeration of sizes, color, space, light that will enhance or redefine ordinary actions or things."[6] From his experience in the advertising world and in producing comic strips, Thiebaud also understood the power of the panel or frame, which inspired his adoption of simplified backgrounds of white or other flat colors in order to isolate his subjects within clearly defined, framed rectangles.

Fig. 27. Georges Seurat (French, 1859–1891), **A Shop and Two Figures**, 1882. Colored crayon on paper, 5⅞ x 9¼ in. Solomon R. Guggenheim Museum, New York, The Hilla Rebay Collection © Solomon R. Guggenheim Foundation, NY

"Public" Drawings

Such focus on drawing's essentials reflects the cultural climate of the 1960s, when visual media came under heightened scrutiny in the age of television and publicity. In *Understanding Media* (1964), philosopher Marshall McLuhan declared that "the medium is the message," while influential art critic Clement Greenberg insisted on reducing art media to the fundamentals. As though responding in advance to what John Berger would surely critique as too much sensory indulgence in his dessert paintings, Thiebaud extracted a syntax of outlines and cross-hatching from their rich impastos to create a black-and-white suite of etchings and aquatints that he titled *Delights* (1964; pls. 10–22). In this group of seventeen prints, Thiebaud celebrated the quality of an etched line. "There's nothing really that I've ever found in other lines that is like an etched line," he notes. "Its fidelity, the richness of it, the density. You just don't get that any other way."[7] Varying the weight of his lines and the direction and density of his gridded hatch-marks, he distills the color and material weight of his paintings into delicate tones of light and shade. The regular mesh applied across *Cake Window* (1964; pl. 20), for example, suggests a transparent pane of glass and creates an allover shimmer. It invites comparison to Georges Seurat's ephemeral sketch of a Parisian shop window (fig. 27), in which Seurat orchestrates a patchwork of horizontal, gestural lines to evoke the luminous screens of the windows and unify the overall field of a commercial display.[8] Whereas Seurat used color to suggest his array of products, Thiebaud varied his methods of cross-hatching to emphasize shadows and articulate forms. *Gum Machine* (1964; pl. 17), from the same suite, makes use of a broad array of graphic effects to capture the transparent globe of the machine and the gumballs within.

Cake Window, from ***Delights*** series (detail, pl. 20), 1964

Presenting all seventeen etchings of *Delights* in book form also enabled Thiebaud to draw upon his experience in film animation and lighting to engage the viewer through shifting points of view. The strongly lit, diagonal composition of *Banana Splits* (1964; pl. 11), for instance, precedes the centralized, open landscape of *Cherry Stand* (1964; pl. 12), while the close-up of *Lemon Meringue* (1964; pl. 18) stands in contrast to the distant, backlit *Dispensers* (1964; pl. 16). Black aquatint generates the playful abstraction of *Suckers* (1964; pl. 19) and provides a final punctuation mark to *Olives* (1964; pl. 22) on a plate.

Not part of the *Delights* suite but certainly related is Thiebaud's *Buffet Table* (1966/1970; pl. 28), a com-

prehensive translation of food motifs in soft pencil. Like the prints, it too refines and reinterprets a painting. It is a virtuosic formal exercise—note the hand-drawn frame—that distills the material weight of his painted imagery into delicate calligraphy, which preserves the individual character of each item, even if some are reduced to graphic symbols.

Extending Thiebaud's exploration of drawing's essentials are other works from the mid-1960s, such as *Tennis Person* (1965; pl. 23) and *Dog* (1967; pl. 29). These, however, were meant to be "public" works that could hang alongside paintings in a gallery and hold their own in an increasingly pluralistic art world. In these, Thiebaud refines the simplified drawing of his "caricatures" with subtle chiaroscuro and elevates his game with Old Master references—from Antonello da Messina's *Virgin Annunciate* (c. 1476) in *Tennis Person* to Diego Velázquez's engaging portraits of animals in *Dog*. The severity and economy of means used to capture these figures, finely rendered against blank backgrounds, responds to the reductive geometry of Minimalism and the mechanical impersonality of Pop and Photorealism, though without relinquishing the human element of empathy. Thiebaud affirms his roots in tradition while engaging the "mind-body" complex, especially in the taut alertness of the dog, which seems to evidence his own intense concentration.

Spatial Tensions

Empathy takes on a spatial character in speculative drawings such as *Toys* (1971; pl. 34), a charcoal drawing created in conjunction with Thiebaud's teaching at the University of California, Davis. There, he challenged students with unconventional arrangements of everyday objects, as though testing pictorial conventions in a laboratory. *Toys* combines the rendering of individual playthings with the depiction of a plane extending into space. Each toy is placed at a corner (there seems to be a rule that each object or its shadow has to touch an edge of the page), which forces the viewer to concentrate on the central emptiness that oscillates between vertical flatness and illusory depth. In the absence of conventional spatial cues, our attention is drawn to the objects in the corners and back and forth across the empty central field, where shadows, the foreshortening of the puppet, and the geometry of the block suggest a view from above.

Such focus on the overall visual field reflects the influence of Gestalt psychologist Rudolf Arnheim, whose ideas were popular with artists in the 1960s but are less well known today. Extending empathy into the realm of compositional forces at work in the visual field, Arnheim holds that we project our bodily awareness of up/down and right/left onto any blank page, inscribing a "hidden architecture" on it prior to its use.[9] Compositional balance or what "feels right," therefore, reflects our personal sense of balance. While Arnheim's internal dynamics remain on the two-dimensional plane and are based in the flat, abstract compositions of modern art, Thiebaud enhances these planar tensions by pushing his subjects into representational space, challenging us to reconcile two-dimensional abstraction with three-dimensional topography and endowing the tabletop with the restless spatiality of his landscapes.

Toys puts the issue of the picture plane—the same flat field that Clement Greenberg championed in Abstract Expressionism and Color Field painting—front and center. For Greenberg, de Kooning's mature "Women" paintings remained rooted in the figural chiaroscuro of Pablo Picasso, whereas Jackson Pollock "literally pulverized value contrasts in a vaporous dust of interfused lights and darks in which every trace of a sculptural effect was obliterated."[10] Greenberg thought Pollock's drips on the floor took painting toward a dematerialized optical realm, which became actualized in the staining or spray-painting of the Color Field painters. Thiebaud, on the other hand, sees drawing in terms of physical empathy: "In order to get it to work, you have to feel it in the pit of your stomach," he says.[11] While Pollock literally exploits the horizontal plane of the floor and incorporates his own bodily movements into the act of painting, Thiebaud incorporates our empathetic imaginations to envision the tabletop, to test the positions of the toys with respect to our own internal plumb line. Pollock is celebrated for breaking boundaries, but Thiebaud has commented that "the boundary is bounded, for me." For Pollock, he argues,

"Space, horizontal, verticals—they're all relative."[12] By contrast, Thiebaud's thumbnail sketches, which are ubiquitous in his "personal" drawings, always establish a stable frame of reference. Thiebaud likes to know where he stands.

In a later drawing, *Man on Table* (1978; pl. 38), Thiebaud lends bodily empathy a macabre twist. Alluding to Andrea Mantegna's *Lamentation over the Dead Christ* (c. 1483; fig. 28), he assumes an eccentric viewpoint (apparently the position he occupied at the session where the drawing was made), placing us at a low angle, from which the table suggests a gurney from a hospital or morgue. It also resembles one of his counter displays but, by being set at an angle, leaves visible only the man's sensitively rendered but abbreviated head and ambiguously articulated hand as points of identification. Thiebaud pays close attention to the mechanics of the table's wheels, while the man's feet are merely suggested. Circular gestures enact the curved volumes of the figure's leg, allowing viewers to trace the body's construction. Unlike Thiebaud's fully rendered charcoal drawings, however, the overall effect in this less formal "public" drawing is that of a work in progress, or a teaching demonstration.

Tactile Light

One night, when reminiscing about a period during World War II when Thiebaud as a serviceman was able to sit in for free on art courses in Los Angeles, he remembered a demanding instructor who made the class use a hard, sharp pencil to render a white object, observing shadows, highlights, and reflections. Even today, Thiebaud recalls with a hint of metaphysical awe that moment when he first grasped an understanding of how to capture light. He also recalls a teacher who taught students how to draw their own hands. Light

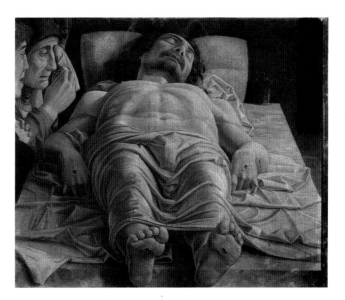

Fig. 28. Andrea Mantegna (Italian, 1431–1506), **Lamentation over the Dead Christ**, c. 1483. Tempera on canvas, 26¾ x 31⅞ in. Pinacoteca di Brera, Milan

and the hand, the visual and manual skills crucial to drawing, therefore merge in his memory with his excitement of learning about the world.[13]

Thiebaud's early training in rendering light was grounded in European academic practice, where dark and light take precedence over color, and a mastery of charcoal is central. In charcoal, the discrete marks of pencil drawing are lost, blended into an overall play of surfaces, within which objects cast shadows and reflect light. Subtle transitions alternate with sharp contrasts to create images that approach the seamless resolution of painting. Even though Thiebaud's use of color can be surprising and inventive—he cites the influence of Pierre Bonnard and Persian miniatures—he prioritizes chiaroscuro: "If you get the value right, the darkness or the lightness, you can then use almost any color, hue, or intensity to fit into that value structure. And that's, I think, a really great human invention."[14] He finds that the success of Henri Matisse's brilliant colors, for instance, rests in the Frenchman's respect for tonal relationships, in which Matisse was well trained, and upon which

Fig. 29. ***Three Ice Cream Cones***, 1964/1986. Sugar lift etching hand-worked with watercolor and gouache, 4⅞ x 4⅞ in. Crocker Art Museum, gift of the artist's family, 1995.9.35

Fig. 30. Edgar Degas (French, 1834–1917), ***The Rehearsal Onstage***, c. 1874. Pastel over brush-and-ink drawing on thin cream-colored wove paper, laid down on bristol board and mounted on canvas, 21 x 28½ in. The Metropolitan Museum of Art, H. O. Havemeyer Collection, Bequest of Mrs. H. O. Havemeyer, 1929, 29.100.39

Thiebaud relies to ground his introduction of pastel, colored pencil, or watercolor. Considering his areas of light and dark first enables Thiebaud to then apply colors with great expressive freedom, as is evidenced by the overall brick red of *Cow Ridge* (n.d.; pl. 64) and the exuberant primary hues of *Bow Ties* (1993; pl. 74).

Thiebaud's signature colored shadows take center stage in *Three Ice Cream Cones* (1964/1986; fig. 29). In this work, saturated hues are applied to dark, backlit cones, as though forcing color into the darkest extreme of the gray scale and pushing the limits of traditional priorities. Such experiments reflect Thiebaud's early experience with lighting on movie and stage sets and

connect him to French Impressionist Edgar Degas. One of Thiebaud's heroes, Degas was fascinated by the artificial lights of the ballet theater and dance hall, just as Thiebaud is by the diner or circus (fig. 30). Degas experimented boldly in mixing media, and his layering of wet and dry media inspired Thiebaud to take similar risks, such as in *Salt Shaker* (1979; pl. 40), a skilled rendering of reflections. Thiebaud's drawing combines watercolor and pastel to generate tactile effects that range from a literal flow of paint to the crystalline hardness of the shaker, the pairing convincing enough to arouse concerns about keeping the salt dry.

Pastel infuses drawing with color. Degas was a master of pastel, his work in this medium a seamless combination of line drawing and nuanced clouds of pigment. Pastels are akin to charcoal in their malleability and richness and, in Thiebaud's hands, approach the accomplishment of his work in oils. Well suited to rendering the moist surface of a watermelon reflected in the sheen of a knife in *Watermelon and Knife* (1989; pl. 63), for instance, they are equally adaptable to other genres, including landscape, such as in the lush

Bow Ties (detail, pl. 74), 1993

Fig. 31. Willem de Kooning (American, b. Netherlands, 1904–1997), **Excavation**, 1950. Oil on canvas, 81 x 100¼ in. The Art Institute of Chicago, Mr. and Mrs. Frank G. Logan Purchase Prize Fund; restricted gifts of Edgar J. Kaufmann Jr., and Mr. and Mrs. Noah Goldowsky, 1952.1. Photograph courtesy The Art Institute of Chicago / Art Resource, NY

calligraphy of *Auburn Hills* (1984; pl. 46). Early on, Thiebaud even created an exercise for himself to draw pastels *with* pastels in *Pastel Scatter* (1972; pl. 35), which sets casual groupings of pastels in syncopated, zig-zag arrangements across an implied tabletop that introduces tension through its recession into space. Thiebaud reports that he worked from memory in creating this work, adjusting the pastels' sizes and positions by intuition, considering equally the effect that they would have on the background and leftover empty space.[15] He did not try to systematically coordinate the foreshortening and sizes of the pastels, instead opting for an irregular interplay among pieces in rhythmic groupings and contrasting directions that are punctuated by colorful fragments. The aim is not so much for overall consistency (the table slopes off to the right) as to engage the viewer in a search for stability. That Thiebaud enhances the tension between planar arrangements and suggestions of depth in a

close-to-the-surface, in-and-out drawing suggests the freedom of de Kooning's famous *Excavation* (1950; fig. 31). The latter is an overall composition seemingly based in Pollock's approach, but one that remains tightly controlled by gestural lines derived from the figure.

Landscapes Made Unfamiliar

Pastel Scatter looks ahead to Thiebaud's landscapes, in which the spatial implications of tabletop overviews in this and other drawings such as *Seven Cupcake Rows* (1995; pl. 80) or *Dark Chocolates* (n.d.; pl. 75) become visceral. In these, the artist's declared intention is to disorient and disturb:

> "I'm not so interested in the pictorial aspect of mountains, as in their abstract potential for expressing some of that feeling of empathy, even to the point of putting us off a bit, or feeling dislocated. That you would feel a sense of disequilibrium. Are you in a helicopter? Or are you on ground level? Well, you're not informed because there's no continuity of unity, of one-eyed view."[16]

Potrero Hill (1989; pl. 65), for instance, inspires vertigo by suspending us high above the ground. Other compositions involve more complex geometries of drawn lines and shaded planes that resort to the old-fashioned device of perspective in order to take the in-and-out drawing of the tabletops to a new level. This more spatial type of drawing differs from his early "caricatures" of objects, as in these he goes back and forth from outdoor observation into the studio to fold "different projective systems into one overall integrated composition."[17] The back-and-forth interplay of abruptly juxtaposed streets often resolves itself around the vertical axis of an uplifted street

Fig. 32. *Wayne Thiebaud discussing pastel landscape drawing as artist Patrick Dullanty demonstrates*, n.d. Photographer unknown

or building, parallel to the vertical plane of our body. The entire composition of *Apartment Hill* (1986; pl. 50), for example, vertiginous as it is, seems reassuringly anchored around the apartment building itself.

Thiebaud's inner urge for stability is also at work in balancing acts like *Park Place* (1995; pl. 79), and in the long, vertical spine of *Central City* (1992; pl. 71). These "integrated compositions," the culmination of the tensely choreographed tabletops, involve the uplifting of the ground plane until it's suspended vertically like a Cubist wall relief, a caricature of space: "Cubism," Thiebaud reasons, "is really a kind of caricature of spatial referents."[18] Efforts at integration could extend even further. Thiebaud reports being "taken" with bas-reliefs on a visit to the Metropolitan Museum of Art in New York, wondering how they could relate to painting: "Is there something in between?" he asks, in reference to his mountains: "These textures in the painting are trying to deal with that a little bit, acting a little like low carvings, or high paintings."[19]

But Thiebaud is not a Cubist, as is apparent from the varied tapestry of life chronicled in his landscapes. The progressive resolution of his cityscapes into Cubist geometry is tempered by his commitment to empathy, which

comes through in his response to all he sees. His carefully observed details resist Cubist formalism, manifesting instead his love of subversive fantasy—as in *Krazy Kat*—as well as in the honesty of folk art and the color and compositions of Indian miniatures. Thiebaud, in fact, faults Synthetic Cubism itself for having been "caricaturized."[20] "They no longer have to look at the model," he explains. "They can just do whatever they want."[21]

While lacking the actual relief of oil impasto, the cityscape etchings do, however, incorporate Thiebaud's abiding sense of physical touch and vertiginous space through a surprising dexterity of media. Finished renderings often include added colors, which don't enhance realism as much as they introduce additional levels of activity. Whereas color is subsidiary to the geometric structure of *Park Place*, the liquid surfaces of *Steep Street* (1993; pl. 76) and *Central* City take on a life of their own. The color etching and aquatint *Steep Street* includes waxed crayon, colored pencil, graphite, and gouache, its regular hatch-marks alternating with loosely applied gestural marks, along with stains and splotches of color. Altogether, it is a richly textured amalgam comparable to the calligraphic richness of the cityscape paintings, a material density that enhances the busy scenes and reinforces their allusions to relief.

Cartoon Memories

As a visual precursor to his cityscapes, Thiebaud likes to recount a memory of a mesa "with stuff on top," near his family's farm in Utah, which his Mormon father struggled to maintain before ultimately moving to California.[22] Thiebaud's later landscapes evidence this memory, just as other recollections are central to his work in different genres. Thiebaud quotes Degas on "the iconic potential of memory" and how memory could provide the basis of style because it "depends on human interjection."[23]

Fig. 33. George Herriman (American, 1880–1944), *Krazy Kat*, March 7, 1943. © King Features Syndicate, Inc.

By conflating these memories with other sources, including, in the realm of landscape at least, the fanciful cartoon landscapes of George Herriman's comic strip *Krazy Kat*, Thiebaud creates the exaggerated but believable crags of mountains and cliffs. He also finds inspiration in Herriman's inventive manipulation of narrative frames (fig. 33). "The graphic power of it [cartooning] still, I think, remains un-researched in a really critical way," Thiebaud opines, "But the iconic power of cartoons . . . needs to be addressed."[24] His *Valley Farm* (1993; pl. 78), for example, recalls

|75|

Valley Farm (detail, pl. 78), 1993

Fig. 34. **Wayne Thiebaud**, c. 1968. Photograph by Betty Jean Thiebaud

Herriman's fantasy landscapes and comes close to the enigmatic diagonal composition that Thiebaud has in turn made iconic. Asserted more radically in *Dark Ridge* (pl. 91), which Thiebaud reworked in three phases in 2010, 2012, and 2019, this diagonal is an imposition of abstraction, a direct extension of the frame. Thiebaud acknowledges that such a bold graphic element doesn't "feel right," but that he nevertheless "can't leave it alone."[25] The corner-to-corner "ridge" might be a landscape (and Thiebaud tries to convince us of this by "landscaping" it, in *Krazy Kat* fashion), yet it is also a cancellation of deep space, a flattening prefigured by Seurat's window displays.[26] Even if it depicts the profile of a hill, the result leaves us in suspense. This, along with the accumulation of gestural marks in the sky and debris on the ground, lends it overtones of a political and environmental apocalypse.

Thumbnails and Diagonals

Thiebaud's explorations of empathy are, of course, based in his engagement with the world around him, which he never stops highlighting. In art generally, the public/private distinction has waned, making it difficult to maintain formal boundaries. Thiebaud contends that he wants to be able to make art "anytime," and of anything that interests him.[27] "I make sketches while visiting different countries, walking in museums, viewing athletic events, riding in the car, listening to concerts, watching television, and attending lectures," he explains.[28] Curator Isabelle Dervaux, who included some twenty sketchbook pages in her survey of Thiebaud's drawings at the Morgan Library and Museum, New York, describes most artists' sketchbook pages as "conceptual field[s] in which figures float freely, jotted down with a total disregard for spatial logic," and yet Thiebaud's are more orderly.[29] If he sometimes renders free and lively groups of intermingling figures in pages like *Untitled (Page of Sketches with Figures and Camels)* (n.d.; pl. 53), the arrangement remains largely linear. He also tends to populate pages with thumbnail sketches—often in boxes—evidence of his concern for the economy of the visual field, the "skin" that bears the image. "This was one of the things I got out of the old art directors who always had you make lots of tiny little compositions before you made a large one," he recalls.[30] Whereas some artists doodle to court the creative impulse, Thiebaud's sketches are more like a musician practicing. He considers them more "neurotic" than playful, justifying them with reference to the many compositional studies that Mondrian made within rectangular grids.[31]

Despite this control, Thiebaud's sketches hold surprises, like the marvelous one of the critic Greenberg (drawn as he lectured on Hans Hofmann), to which Thiebaud juxtaposed brightly colored candied apples (1986; pl. 51). Another such drawing, *Untitled (Page of*

Sketches with Candied Apples and Watermelon Slices) (early 1980s; pl. 44), stops us cold with its crisp framing and powerful relief. The knife stabbing the soft watermelon and the sensory appeal of the candy-coated apples arouse an immediate bodily response. The candied apples' sticks in their dark-and-light arrays also echo the verticality of the knife, while the watermelon slice establishes a centralized composition like the reliefs of the cityscapes. The flat background also comes into focus like those in the still lifes, rather than as the vague "conceptual field" that Dervaux describes.

Though supposedly preparatory, such a page of sketches can hold its own next to Thiebaud's "public" drawings, as his design sense is so ingrained. "I feel like I always have an art director over my shoulder," he jokes.[32] Although a small drawing, it is nevertheless emblematic of a wider range of media and the artist's contention that art is a metaphor for the body, proving that even a small work of modest subject matter can be an expression of empathy, conveying implications that belie its apparent commonality and scale. ▲▼▲

NOTES

1. Wayne Thiebaud, "Wayne Thiebaud: 'The Painted World'," Elson Lecture, March 1, 2000, National Gallery of Art, Washington, DC, podcast, 47:29, https://www.nga.gov/audio-video /audio/elson-thiebaud.html.

2. Wayne Thiebaud, quoted in Isabelle Dervaux, *Wayne Thiebaud: Draftsman* (New York: Morgan Library and Museum, 2018), 148.

3. John Berger, *Ways of Seeing* (London: Penguin Books, 1972), 93.

4. Wayne Thiebaud, quoted in Hearne Pardee, "Wayne Thiebaud with Hearne Pardee," *Brooklyn Rail* (March 2019).

5. Adam Gopnik, "An American Painter," in *Wayne Thiebaud: A Paintings Retrospective,* by Steven A. Nash and Adam Gopnik (San Francisco: Fine Arts Museums of San Francisco, 2000), 49.

6. Thiebaud, quoted in Dervaux, *Draftsman*, 149.

7. Wayne Thiebaud, quoted on "Wayne Thiebaud" (web page), Crown Point Press, accessed December 20, 2019, https://crownpoint.com/artist /wayne-thiebaud/.

8. Jonathan Crary, *Suspensions of Perception: Attention, Spectacle, and Modern Culture* (Cambridge, MA: MIT Press, 1999), 195.

9. Rudolf Arnheim, *Art and Visual Perception: A Psychology of the Creative Eye* (Berkeley, CA: University of California Press, 1966), 3–4.

10. Clement Greenberg, "'American-Type' Painting," in Clement Greenberg, *Art and Culture: Critical Essays* (Boston: Beacon Press, 1961), 228.

11. Wayne Thiebaud, quoted in Gopnik, "An American Painter," 58.

12. Wayne Thiebaud, quoted in Eve Aschheim and Chris Daubert, *Episodes with Wayne Thiebaud: Four Interviews 2009–2011* (New York: Black Square Editions, 2014), 29.

13. Wayne Thiebaud, interview with the author, June 28, 2019.

14. Thiebaud, quoted in Pardee, "Wayne Thiebaud with Hearne Pardee."

15. Thiebaud, quoted in Aschheim and Daubert, *Episodes*, 36–37.

16. Thiebaud, quoted in Pardee, "Wayne Thiebaud with Hearne Pardee."

17. Thiebaud, quoted in Dervaux, *Draftsman*, 149.

18. Thiebaud, quoted in Pardee, "Wayne Thiebaud with Hearne Pardee."

19. Thiebaud, quoted in Pardee, "Wayne Thiebaud with Hearne Pardee."

20. Thiebaud, quoted in Pardee, "Wayne Thiebaud with Hearne Pardee."

21. Thiebaud, quoted in Pardee, "Wayne Thiebaud with Hearne Pardee."

22. Thiebaud, quoted in Aschheim and Daubert, *Episodes*, 47.

23. Thiebaud, quoted in Pardee, "Wayne Thiebaud with Hearne Pardee."

24. Thiebaud, quoted in Pardee, "Wayne Thiebaud with Hearne Pardee."

25. Thiebaud, quoted in Pardee, "Wayne Thiebaud with Hearne Pardee."

26. Crary, *Suspensions of Perception*, 195.

27. Thiebaud, quoted in Pardee, "Wayne Thiebaud with Hearne Pardee."

28. Wayne Thiebaud, quoted in Laurie S. Hurwitz, "Wayne Thiebaud's Studied Sensuality," *American Artist* 57, no. 615 (October 1993): 29–30.

29. Dervaux, *Draftsman*, 111.

30. Wayne Thiebaud, quoted in Alessia Masi, "Interview to Wayne Thiebaud," *Wayne Thiebaud at Museo Morandi* (Mantua, Italy: Corraini Edizioni, 2011), 47.

31. Thiebaud, quoted in Masi, "Interview to Wayne Thiebaud," 47.

32. Wayne Thiebaud, interview with the author, June 28, 2019.

4

NOTHING IS UNIMPORTANT

Julia Friedman

If you find yourself able to make people laugh, it is God's gift. You have to do everything from the bottom of your heart. I don't go in for slapstick. I let the emotion come from inside and penetrate the eyes. I am the same man underneath, I'm always part of the human tragi-comedy.

—Otto Griebling (1962)[1]

It is paradoxical that Wayne Thiebaud—a quintessential "how" painter—is regularly introduced by the "what" of his paintings. Despite his status as an "artist's artist," Thiebaud's wider audience associates his work with the everyday subject matter he made iconic: desserts, streetscapes, and mountains. By depicting such vernacular and even clichéd objects afresh, Thiebaud succeeded at the elusive task of creating a new visual species, a new (painted) world. Unfortunately, this success has also created a persistent focus on his subject matter and its ontological attributes at the expense of the paintings' formal qualities. Partly due to the coincidence in the timing of Thiebaud's decision to base his still lifes on the objects and foodstuffs from window displays and supermarket shelves, and the rise of New York Pop artists—Andy Warhol, Roy Lichtenstein, and James Rosenquist—Thiebaud's paintings from the early 1960s landed in the Pop Art pigeonhole. Thiebaud's commercial art background notwithstanding, he has long disagreed with this fundamental mis-categorization, seeing his origins in painting, not in design—the root of American Pop.

As far as he is concerned, the subject matter is at most a philosophical entry point into a painting, where the emphasis is not on the "what" but on the "how."

Thiebaud's good friend and University of California colleague, British philosopher Richard Wollheim, warned against the fallacy of prioritizing subject matter: "What the artist's work expresses is not the same as what the work represents, narrates, depicts; it is not subject-matter, but rather the attitudes, emotions, feelings, encouraged toward subject-matter."[2] Wollheim's insistence on the inherent complexity of the artist's varied mental states, which are at once "highly structured" and "highly elusive," arises from the idea that a creative activity such as painting can become a process of self-knowledge.[3] His view is aligned with Thiebaud's, who believes that painting "allow[s] us to see ourselves looking at ourselves," to "applaud or criticize what is especially us." Thiebaud made this comment in the summer of 1962 when the *San Francisco Chronicle* asked for a statement to be used in a review of his solo exhibition at the M. H. de Young Memorial Museum.[4]

Clown with Red Hair (detail, pl. 93), 2015

While Thiebaud addressed his choice of subject matter in the statement's introduction, it is clear that his interests were, above all, formal. These interests did not change in the nearly six decades that have elapsed since: the four sections of Thiebaud's practical yet sophisticated account—"Light," "Space," "Color," and "Philosophic Viewpoint"—correspond to categories that came up in many of our conversations over eighteen months in which we discussed his clown memories and the new body of work that came out of them.

Thiebaud began his latest series of paintings and drawings five years ago, and it is presently his main artistic focus. Based on the artist's recollections of a traveling circus he encountered in Long Beach, California, in the early 1930s, the series is a palimpsest of events from the past and his concerns of the present. It is informed by a lifetime of painting, looking at art, reading about art, teaching studio classes, and lecturing. It revisits childhood memories with the hindsight of adult wisdom, as well as a clearheaded understanding of our current age, with its absurdist politics and performative, digitally overshared lives.

After decades of exhibiting his work, Thiebaud developed a good sense for what American viewers need: uplifting, redemptive art that relies on humor rather than unnecessary thematic complexity and gratuitous gloom. Thiebaud's paintings leave smiles on people's faces. *Bumping Clowns* (2016; pl. 94), for example, downplays the prospect of injury, even as two flying clowns are about to smash their red noses in midair, and an excruciating collision appears imminent. An avid tennis player, Thiebaud based the clowns' improbable act on the Bryan brothers' famous chest bump—an affectionate fraternal gesture between doubles tennis partners.

Yet, for all their redemptive and uplifting character, Thiebaud's clown paintings are also a somber commentary on the human condition. They parody our

simulacrum-infused reality, in which old-fashioned circuses are all but gone because they are too slow-paced for a generation whose attention span was recalibrated by television. Like the "banal" objects of his early still lifes, Thiebaud's recent paintings of clowns are a path to self-knowledge precisely because they "allow us to see ourselves looking at ourselves," to "applaud or criticize what is especially us."[5] The late nineteenth- and early twentieth-century three-ring circus, in which the audience reacted in unison to the performers, has been since replaced by individuals solitarily entertained by personal electronic devices. Today, the sideshow acts and "freak shows" have migrated into street fashion, where vibrantly hued hair, oversized pants, and bulky shoes mimic the clown costumes of yore; and where regular citizens vie for the opportunity to reveal their phobias and peccadilloes before an audience of strangers on YouTube, reality TV, and tabloid talk shows. Clowns are no longer caricatures of people but their avatars, ritually performing the human condition in the format of a circus show: a succession of tragicomic acts followed by the Great Egress—a promised final attraction that turns out to be the Exit.

Clowns have popped up in Thiebaud's work before, but this time he approaches the subject more systematically. He does so with great care and sensitivity to the long tradition of clowns represented in Western painting. Clowns and their cousins—Pierrots, Harlequins, Bajazzos, Pulcinelli, mountebanks, Badins, jesters, tramps, zanies—have occupied artists' imagination for well over three hundred years. Antoine Watteau, Claude Gillot, Domenico Tiepolo, Francisco Goya, Honoré Daumier, Gustave Courbet, Georges Seurat, James Ensor, Henri de Toulouse-Lautrec, Georges Rouault, Pablo Picasso, André Derain, Gino Severini, Max Beckmann, Edward Hopper, and Walt Kuhn all painted and drew clowns. They invested clowns with various associations, from surrogates for the artist's position vis-à-vis the public, to faith in fallible humanity, to a profoundly pessimistic view of human deficiency. Clowns have been used to express bohemian aloofness and presented as multivalent and mysterious; they have also been depicted as timeless, isolated and alienated, supernatural and demonic, miraculous and crepuscular, ordinary and marvelous. Thiebaud, who is well aware of these interpretational complexities, doesn't seem concerned with the most recent, and plentiful, incarnations of the clown in contemporary art. Chronologically, Beckmann and Kuhn are his latest points of visual reference.

Within the series, Thiebaud's own memories of the circus are interwoven with its representations in film and literature, each source containing multiple levels of meaning. Just one such critical influence on Thiebaud's clown paintings, Henry Miller's 1948 novella about a clown, *The Smile at the Foot of the Ladder* (fig. 37), exposes the relationship of the series to aesthetics, existentialist philosophy, Jungian psychology, literary criticism, historiography of clowns, and theology. Fascinating as these contextual connections are, however, I am compelled to take Thiebaud's words that "the paintings speak better for themselves" at face value and dedicate the rest of this essay to the discussion of the series's "specific esthetic and philosophic problems," mirroring the structure of the painter's 1962 statement for the *San Francisco Chronicle* (fig. 35).[6]

Light: Most of the clown paintings present the strong, evenly distributed glare of commercial lighting, which Thiebaud has been depicting for decades and has described as enabling "all kinds of goofy and wonderful things."[7] The most distinct kind of light in this series appears as the circular spotlight shone onto the figures in the center ring. The spotlight has a higher value at the center, gradient color toward the edge, and

Fig. 35. "Is a Lollipop Tree Worth Painting?" *San Francisco Chronicle*, July 15, 1962. Image courtesy of Timothy O'Rourke, Hearst Newspapers

a darker core with or without an outline. The areas of higher value make objects within it cast colorful shadows and create impasto halos.

In two of the paintings a spotlight is cast in reverse. In both cases, the clowns appear to teeter on the front edge of the dark circle. The elliptical shape doubles as a gaping chasm into which the clown might fall, presumably to the amusement of the audience. The duality of this light is important, as it contributes to the ambiguity that permeates the series on every level. In *Clown and Shadow* (2015; fig. 36), a little potbellied figure, roughly one-sixth the size of the square he inhabits, appears to lean to the left of the central axis—an effect created by the improbable purple shadow that starts at his feet and continues on the foreshortened diagonal toward the right margin of the canvas. But, in actuality, the clown's red nose is right in the center of the painting—a compositional fact thrown into doubt by light and color.

Several works, including his *Clown Angel and Dog* (2017; pl. 96)—an enigmatic painting of a winged clown welcoming a seated dog with outstretched arms— feature a shimmering, pearly light.[8] The glint of this

Fig. 36. ***Clown and Shadow***, 2015. Oil on board, 11¾ x 11⅜ in. Courtesy of Paul Thiebaud Gallery, San Francisco. Photograph by Phocasso / J. W. White

Clown Boots (detail, pl. 97), 2018/2019

painting's surface surrounds the clown, and the white background is perforated with tiny gouges and a rise of scar-like accretions. These surface elements suggest Thiebaud's fondness for simultaneity by giving optical, physical expression to a metaphysical concept. According to the painter, such optical manifestations of simultaneity might be the perfect expression of the most haunting aspect of clowns, whom he sees as humans and phantoms at once, as these surface elements allow him "to work out what is most memorable about the subject at hand and get it down."[9]

Space: The same gauge and accretion marks used to designate light in *Clown Angel and Dog* double as what Thiebaud calls directional points or vectors, creating a "secondary space" different from the fictional space of the painting. Overall, the treatment of space seems to be determined by the amount of action on the part of the subjects. Some circus acts require contextual surroundings such as the arena, bumpers, curtain, or spotlight. The flat picture plane is moderated by the illusion of volumetric spatial references, adding a touch of plausibility. Such isolation of objects is a familiar and purposeful trope in Thiebaud's work. Like the confections of his early still lifes, the isolated figures in the clown series activate the space around them. The focus here seems to be on the variety of textured and smooth surfaces. The ambiguity of the transitions between smooth and bas-relief portions of the paintings produces tension, which is at times reinforced by physical discrepancies, making the viewer aware of space. Such is the case in his 2016 *Clown and Makeup* (fig. 24, p. 49), a clash between a diagonally tilted clown, naked from the waist up, and the horizontal, flat stripe of counter behind which he sits.

Color: Thiebaud opens the "Color" section of his 1962 statement with: "I don't think I am much of a colorist."[10] He went on to clarify that he was more interested in intense contrasts, because they conveyed his concern with the idea of starkness and glare. In the circus series, where ambiguity and a multivalent potential for meaning are central, the color is no longer characterized by intense contrasts but by a spectral, contiguous quality. Many of the clowns have ombré costumes, and even such elements as striped socks are mitigated by gradient shading between the stripes. The idea that things are not what they seem is reinforced, for instance, in *Clown and Shadow* (2015; fig. 36), wherein the clown's costume and body blend into one: his red nose continues along an arc of red buttons going up his prosthetic (or real?) belly; his rainbow makeup blends into his suit. The artifice of his made-up face and lobsterlike red hands emphasizes the resemblance of the costume to a bodysuit, so that the clown, though man-shaped, comes across more as a figurine than a figure.

There is a familiar Fauve element in many of these paintings, in which complementary colors set each other off. Thiebaud's recognizable palette of intense yellows, oranges, and blues is supplemented by mid-value hues

evocative of those popular during the Great Depression. The *Clown with Red Hair* (2015; pl. 93), for example, is placed in front of a crimson curtain that provides a dark background for his rose-colored shirt and heavily patched, ill-fitting olive trousers. These Depression-era colors are enhanced by chronologically appropriate lighting: many of the paintings in the series capture the dim, yellow glow of the incandescent lamps that dominated American interiors before fluorescent lighting became common in consumer goods displays, a reference, perhaps, to Thiebaud's childhood of the 1920s and early '30s.

Philosophic Viewpoint: Paintings of clowns and their acts manifest a breadth of human experience: work, play, joy, sadness, failure, friendship, surrender, and death. In his 1976 monograph on the history of clowns, circus historian John H. Towsen recounts the centuries-long tradition of clowns as performers who dramatize commonplace activities: the clown act exaggerates the mundane.[11] Clowns *pretend* to carry out human actions in the extreme, allowing for *virtual* possibilities, while at the same time only getting into imaginary trouble.

Clown acts, in their suspension of disbelief, are akin to cartoons and comic strips in which subjects miraculously survive being incinerated, smashed, or blown up. Thiebaud's early career as a cartoonist, and his lifelong dedication to the genre, eases the burden of verisimilitude in his paintings, as is the case with the aforementioned *Bumping Clowns* (pl. 94). The suggestion of infinite possibilities in the clown series points to a key source for this body of work: the comic art of George Herriman, whose influence Thiebaud has acknowledged on more than one occasion.[12] Herriman's logic-defying, daily comic strip *Krazy Kat* (fig. 33, p. 75) is an inspiration for Thiebaud's illusory clown acts, and not just as cartoons, but as artworks *sui generis*. A decade into its run in the mid-1920s, art critic Gilbert Seldes called *Krazy Kat* "the most amusing and fantastic and satisfactory artwork produced in America today."[13] Sixty years later, another art critic—conservative essayist Hilton Kramer—recognized begrudgingly that because the boundaries between popular culture and fine arts "have shifted so radically . . . the *Krazy Kat* drawings are likely to look more like classics than a good many paintings and sculptures that are nowadays on view."[14] Thiebaud's clown series echoes *Krazy Kat's* reliance on irony and fantasy in a fine-arts version of a "genuine, honest native product."[15]

A clown's efficacy is predicated on their interaction with spectators, similar to the way paintings need viewers. Clowns come into existence through the act of performance, just as painters are nurtured by recognition of their work. Yet, Thiebaud, who holds the rare distinction of being both a great painter and a popular one, is acutely aware of the dangers lurking in renown. Keeping in mind the trials-by-fame of the sad clown Baptiste Debureau from Marcel Carné's 1945 movie classic *Les énfants du paradis*, Thiebaud never settles for a formula, no matter how successful. His continuous personal and creative search has clear parallels in Miller's *The Smile at the Foot of the Ladder*, which Thiebaud acknowledges as a seminal influence on his clown paintings and which describes clowns as "poets in action."[16] In his search for contentment, the protagonist of Miller's story, the celebrated clown Auguste, goes through a series of personal transformations as he comes to realize that artistic fame is the ultimate trap: an idolized artist becomes separated from his fellow men. Auguste's newly found aim is to unify the transcendent life of an artist with being a man, like others, "doing all the foolish, trifling, necessary things which others did."[17] "Because," Auguste expounds,

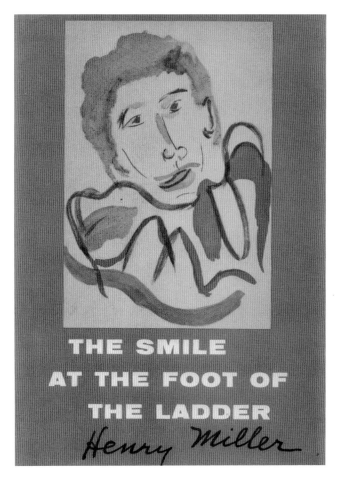

Fig. 37. Cover of Henry Miller's ***The Smile at the Foot of the Ladder***, 1958. © New Directions Publishing

"nothing is unimportant. Nothing. Instead of laughter and applause you will receive smiles. Contented little smiles—that's all. But it's everything . . . more than one could ask for."[18] It is a sentiment that Thiebaud shares.

Miller warns against the complacency of isolating oneself in the world of art in order to avoid a life of action. "The circus," he explains in the story's epilogue, "is a tiny closed off arena of forgetfulness" that "enables us to lose ourselves, to dissolve in wonder and bliss," avoiding "the old everyday world with which we imagine ourselves to be only too familiar."[19] The irony of life is that its stages are mere prototypes: "Like a clown, we go through the motions, forever simulating, forever postponing the grand event. We die struggling to get born."[20] This existentialist stance is echoed in Thiebaud's recognition that "none of us can escape our responsibility however totalitarian or utopian our world may be."[21] Though here referencing still lifes of window displays and store counters, these words nonetheless emphasize that no matter the importance of painting, the artist must remain anchored in reality and not give in to the temptation of self-dissolution, neither through the wonder and bliss of painting nor the adulation of the art world.

To embrace life in its complexity requires acknowledging—and reconciling—the extremes of comedy and tragedy that are the fabric of life, a challenge that was met by Thiebaud's clown paintings. Of the entire series, this concept of the tragicomic is best represented in *Clown Boots* (2018/2019; pl. 97), which depicts a pair of anthropomorphic high tops, their fronts respectively sporting a comic and a tragic clown face. The painting references Vincent van Gogh's famous portrait of a pair of shoes and alludes to Miller's own illustration for his story, which portrays a clown with two mouths, "one for joy and one for sorrow"—the tragicomic (fig. 37).[22] Tragicomedy is key to the clown series because the circus is the ultimate tragicomic world—a union of two oppositions, of seriousness and merriment in which one attempts to resolve absurdity through "silent, . . . mirthless laughter."[23]

Only three years after Thiebaud's 1962 solo show at the de Young, in a textbook instance of zeitgeist happenstance, American philosophy professor Albert Hofstadter published an article titled "The Tragicomic: Concern in Depth." In it, Hofstadter presented the tragicomedy as more than a combination of tragic and comic, insisting that the two are mutually determining, and that the tragicomic "is a genuine living union of opposites."[24] He cited playwright Eugène Ionesco's *The New Tenant*, a 1953 play in which characters are overwhelmed by furniture during an apartment move, as an example of harmonious contrast between the unserious ("levity of concern") and the serious ("gravity of concern"). The origins of Ionesco's tragicomic play, in his view, were in "the consciousness of evanescence, emptiness, light, and the unreal transparency of the world, and the consciousness of solidity, too much presence, darkness, and the opacity of the world"—a description that echoes the duality of Thiebaud's human/phantom clowns.[25] While Hofstadter recognizes that laughter is a natural response to absurdity, he also acknowledges that the comic retreat into ontological space is a compromise, not a victory. The philosopher's clarion call is to counteract absurdity through the tragicomic by introducing a "fumbling inefficacy in facing reality" as well as "a tender warmth of humanity," both doubling as a summons to Thiebaud's messianic clowns.[26]

The "bright pathos" of the circus paintings also finds a parallel in Hofstadter's definition of the tragicomic as an equilibrium, a funambulist act.[27] This is an act that Thiebaud has been performing at least since he had to justify to the *San Francisco Chronicle* that a lollipop tree was worth painting.[28] Then and now—however comical the subject matter—Thiebaud has always taken its representation and his craft as a painter with utmost seriousness. His humble attitude, meanwhile, is mimicked in this chapter's epigraph containing the words of Otto Griebling, a famous tramp clown who, like Thiebaud in his clown series, drew his material from Depression-era Americana: "I am the same man underneath, I'm always part of the human tragi-comedy."[29] ▲▼▲

Bumping Clowns (detail, pl. 94), 2016

NOTES

1. Otto Griebling, quoted in John H. Towsen, *Clowns* (New York: Hawthorn Books, 1976), 304.

2. Richard Wollheim, *The Mind and Its Depths* (Cambridge, MA: Harvard University Press, 1993), 8.

3. Wollheim, *The Mind*, 11.

4. Wayne Thiebaud, "Is a Lollipop Tree Worth Painting?" *San Francisco Sunday Chronicle*, July 15, 1962. The *Chronicle* noted that Thiebaud's written statement was "so interesting and so inclusive" that, instead of publishing a proper review, they ran the text in its entirety.

5. Thiebaud, "Lollipop Tree?"

6. Thiebaud, "Lollipop Tree?"

7. Thiebaud, "Lollipop Tree?"

8. The notion of the angelic clown features prominently in Henry Miller's *The Smile at the Foot of the Ladder*. In the epilogue, Miller mentions the 1943 book *Clowns and Angels* by his friend and correspondent scholar Wallace Fowlie, who also wrote about Miller's work (New York: Sheed and Ward). Henry Miller, *The Smile at the Foot of the Ladder* (New York; New Directions Publishing, 1974), 44. For more on Miller's use of clown/angel trope see Karl Orend, *Henry Miller's Angelic Clown: Reflections on* "The Smile at the Foot of the Ladder" (Paris: Alyscamps Press, 2007).

9. Thiebaud, "Lollipop Tree?"

10. Thiebaud, "Lollipop Tree?"

11. Towsen, *Clowns*, 3–6. Similarly, clown Auguste, the protagonist of Miller's novella, says of the circus acts that "it was his special privilege to reenact the errors, the follies, the stupidities, and all the misunderstandings which plague human kind."; Miller, *Smile*, 29.

12. He also painted sets for the San Francisco Ballet's 1990 production of *Krazy Kat* and contributed to the Campbell-Thiebaud Gallery's *Homage to George Herriman* exhibition curated by Bill Berkson in 1997.

13. Gilbert Seldes, "The Krazy Kat That Walks by Himself" in *Krazy Kat: The Comic Art of George Herriman*, by Patrick McDonnell, Karen O'Connell, and Georgia Riley de Havenon (New York: Harry N. Abrams, 1986), 13.

14. Hilton Kramer, "Art," *New York Times*, January 17, 1982.

15. Seldes, "The Krazy Kat," 15.

16. Miller, *Smile,* 46. Thiebaud knew Miller personally, having met him through his daughter Twinka Thiebaud, who was Miller's friend, assistant, and caretaker. In 2011, Eio Books published *What Doncha Know? about Henry Miller*—Twinka Thiebaud's book of memoirs about Miller.

17. Miller, *Smile*, 20.

18. Miller, *Smile*, 23.

19. Miller, *Smile*, 48.

20. Miller, *Smile*, 48.

21. Thiebaud, "Lollipop Tree?"

22. Miller, *Smile*, 46.

23. Miller, *Smile*, 47.

24. Albert Hofstadter, "The Tragicomic: Concern in Depth," *Journal of Aesthetics and Art Criticism* 24, no. 2 (Winter 1965): 295–302, 295.

25. Hofstadter, "The Tragicomic," 296.

26. Hofstadter, "The Tragicomic," 298.

27. Wayne Thiebaud, notes on circus memories, author archive.

28. Thiebaud, "Lollipop Tree?"

29. Griebling, in Towsen, *Clowns*, 304.

PLATES

1. *Self-Portrait*, 1947. Oil on paper, 16¹³⁄₁₆ x 13⅛ in. Courtesy of the artist

2. *The Sea Rolls In*, 1958. Oil on canvas, 36½ x 47 in. Crocker Art Museum Purchase, 1958.5

3. *Zither Player*, 1959. Oil on canvas, 28 x 24⅛ in. Courtesy of the artist

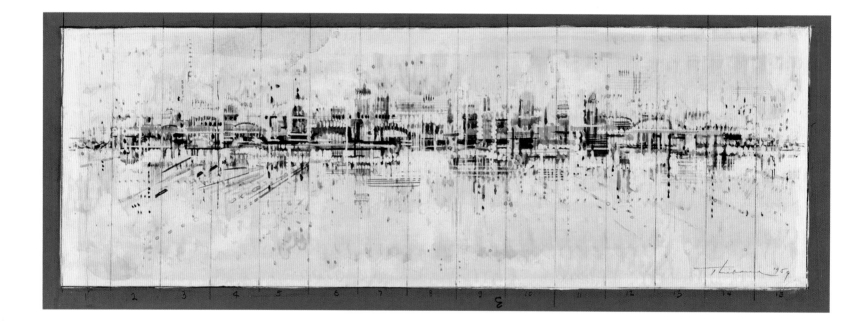

4. *Water City (Preliminary Rendering for SMUD Mural)*, 1959. Watercolor, pencil, and gouache on board, 6¾ x 17⅛ in.
Crocker Art Museum, gift of Paul E. Shaad, 1986.11

5. *Cold Cereal*, 1961. Oil on canvas, 24⅛ x 30⅛ in. Courtesy of the artist

6. *Hamburger*, 1961. Oil on canvas, 12 x 16 in. Collection of Paul LeBaron Thiebaud Trust

7. *Three Prone Figures*, 1961. Oil on canvas, 14 x 18 in. Collection of Paul LeBaron Thiebaud Trust

8. *Pies, Pies, Pies*, 1961. Oil on canvas, 20 x 30 in. Crocker Art Museum, gift of Philip L. Ehlert in memory of Dorothy Evelyn Ehlert, 1974.12

9. *Boston Cremes*, 1962. Oil on canvas, 14 x 18 in. Crocker Art Museum Purchase, 1964.22

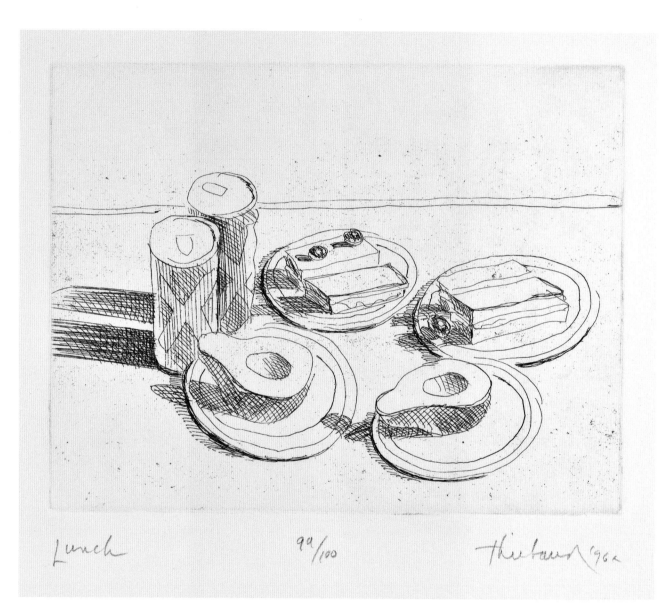

Lunch   99/100   Thiebaud '64

10. *Lunch*, from *Delights* series, 1964. Etching, 5 x 6¹¹⁄₁₆ in. (plate); 12¾ x 10¾ in. (sheet).
Crocker Art Museum, gift of the artist's family, 1995.9.1.1

Banana Splits   99/100   Thiebaud 1964

11. *Banana Splits*, from *Delights* series, 1964. Etching, 3⅞ x 4¹³⁄₁₆ in. (plate); 12¾ x 10¾ in. (sheet).
Crocker Art Museum, gift of the artist's family, 1995.9.1.3

Cherry Stand   99/100   Thiebaud '64

12. *Cherry Stand*, from *Delights* series, 1964. Etching, 5¹¹⁄₁₆ x 6¹³⁄₁₆ in. (plate); 12¾ x 10¾ in. (sheet).
Crocker Art Museum, gift of the artist's family, 1995.9.1.4

Bacon & Eggs   99/100   Thiebaud '964

13. *Bacon and Eggs*, from ***Delights*** series, 1964. Etching, 5¹⁄₁₆ x 5⁵⁄₁₆ in. (plate); 12¾ x 10¾ in. (sheet).
Crocker Art Museum, gift of the artist's family, 1995.9.1.5

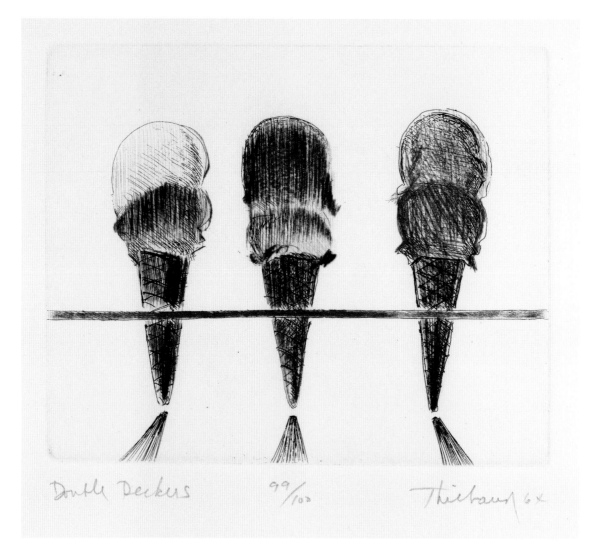

Double Deckers   99/100   Thiebaud 6×

14. *Double Deckers*, from ***Delights*** series, 1964. Drypoint, 3¹⁵⁄₁₆ x 4⅞ in. (plate); 12¾ x 10¾ in. (sheet).
Crocker Art Museum, gift of the artist's family, 1995.9.1.6

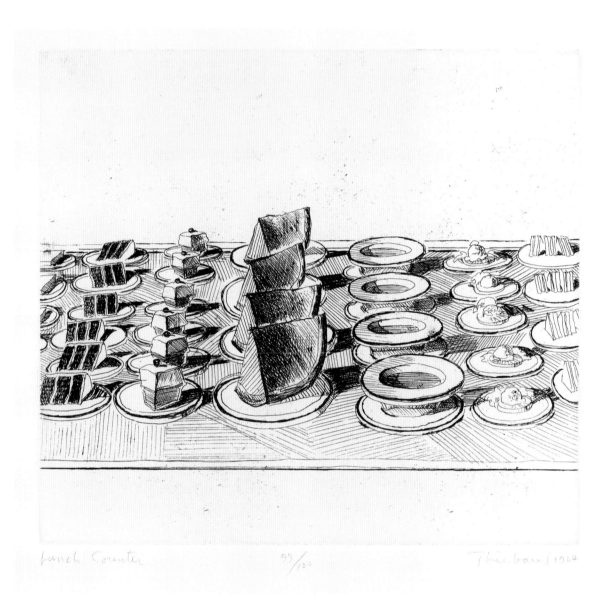

15. *Lunch Counter*, from *Delights* series, 1964. Etching, 5 x 6¹¹⁄₁₆ in. (plate); 12¾ x 10¾ in. (sheet).
Crocker Art Museum, gift of the artist's family, 1995.9.1.7

16. *Dispensers*, from *Delights* series, 1964. Etching, 3⅞ x 4⅞ in. (plate); 12¾ x 10¾ in. (sheet).
Crocker Art Museum, gift of the artist's family, 1995.9.1.8

Gum Machine   99/100   Thiebaud 64

17. *Gum Machine*, from *Delights* series, 1964. Etching, 3⅞ x 3⅞ in. (plate); 12¾ x 10¾ in. (sheet).
Crocker Art Museum, gift of the artist's family, 1995.9.1.9

Lemon Meringue   99/100   Thiebaud 1964

18. *Lemon Meringue*, from **Delights** series, 1964. Etching, 3⅞ x 4⅞ in. (plate); 12¾ x 10¾ in. (sheet).
Crocker Art Museum, gift of the artist's family, 1995.9.1.10

Suckers   99/100   Thiebaud 1964

19. *Suckers*, from *Delights* series, 1964. Aquatint, 4$\frac{15}{16}$ x 4$\frac{7}{8}$ in. (plate); 12$\frac{3}{4}$ x 10$\frac{3}{4}$ in. (sheet).
Crocker Art Museum, gift of the artist's family, 1995.9.1.11

20. *Cake Window*, from ***Delights*** series, 1964. Etching, 4¹⁵⁄₁₆ x 5⅞ in. (plate); 12¾ x 10¾ in. (sheet).
Crocker Art Museum, gift of the artist's family, 1995.9.1.13

Pies   99/10.   Thiebaud 1964

21. *Pies*, from *Delights* series, 1964. Aquatint, 3⅞ x 4⅞ in. (plate); 12¾ x 10¾ in. (sheet).
Crocker Art Museum, gift of the artist's family, 1995.9.1.15

Olives   99/100   Thiebaud 1964

22. *Olives*, from ***Delights*** series, 1964. Aquatint, 2⅞ x 3⅞ in. (plate); 12¾ x 10¾ in. (sheet).
Crocker Art Museum, gift of the artist's family, 1995.9.1.17

23. *Tennis Person*, 1965. Graphite on illustration board, 8¹⁵⁄₁₆ x 7⅞ in. Courtesy of the artist

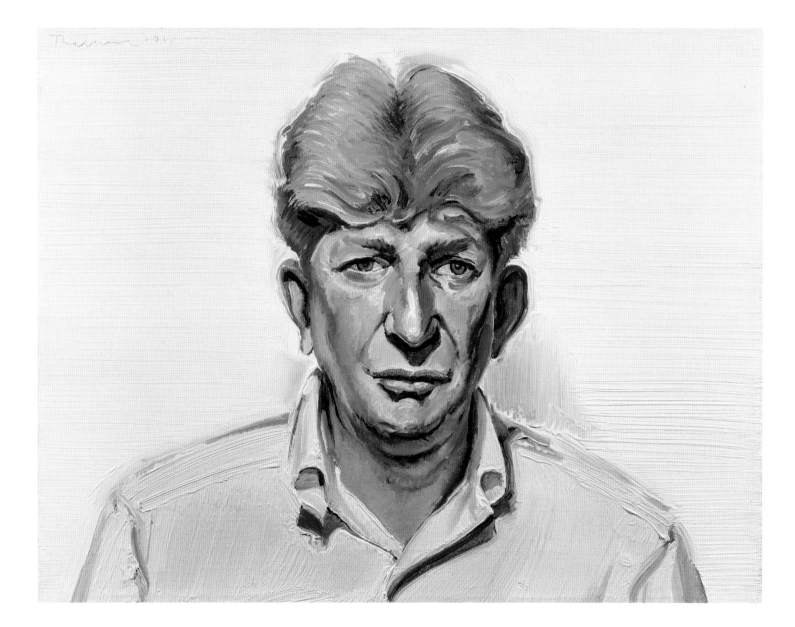

24. *Portrait of Sterling Holloway*, 1965. Oil on canvas, 17¹⁄₁₆ x 22¼ in. Courtesy of the artist

25. *Betty Jean Thiebaud and Book*, 1965–1969. Oil on canvas, 36 x 30 in. Crocker Art Museum, gift of Mr. and Mrs. Wayne Thiebaud, 1969.21

26. *Two Seated Figures*, 1965. Oil on canvas, 60 x 72 in. Courtesy of the Wayne Thiebaud Foundation

27. *Swimsuit Figures*, 1966. Oil on canvas, 72 x 30½ in. Courtesy of the artist

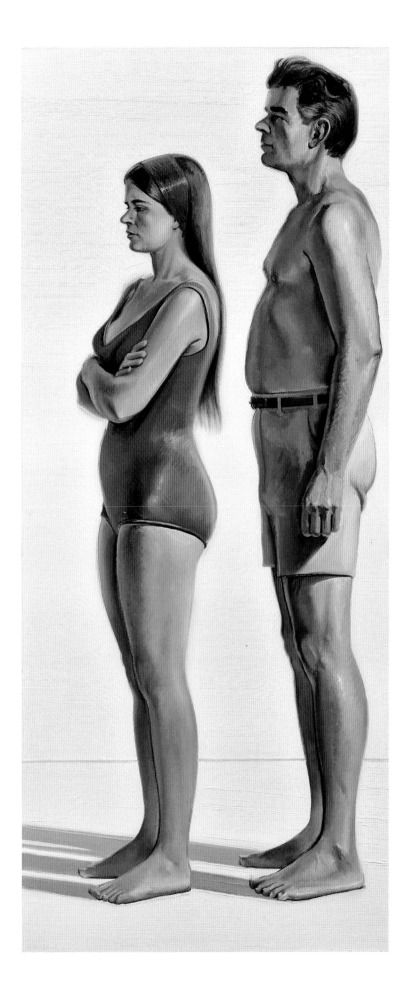

28. *Buffet Table*, 1966/1970. Graphite on paper, 8½ x 11 in. (sheet). Crocker Art Museum, gift of the artist's family, 1995.9.9

29. *Dog*, 1967. Graphite on paper, 9⅛ x 7⅛ in. Courtesy of the artist

30. *Six Candied Apples*, 1968. Lithograph, 16 x 22 in. (sheet). Crocker Art Museum, Estate of Roger and Lenore Stokes, 1992.4.7

31. *Strawberry Cone*, 1969. Oil on paper mounted on board, 11 x 14 in. Courtesy of the artist

32. *Masks*, 1970. Oil on canvas, 24 x 23⅞ in. Courtesy of the artist

33. *Window View*, 1971/1981. Oil on linen, 7¾ x 11⅝ in. Courtesy of the Wayne Thiebaud Foundation

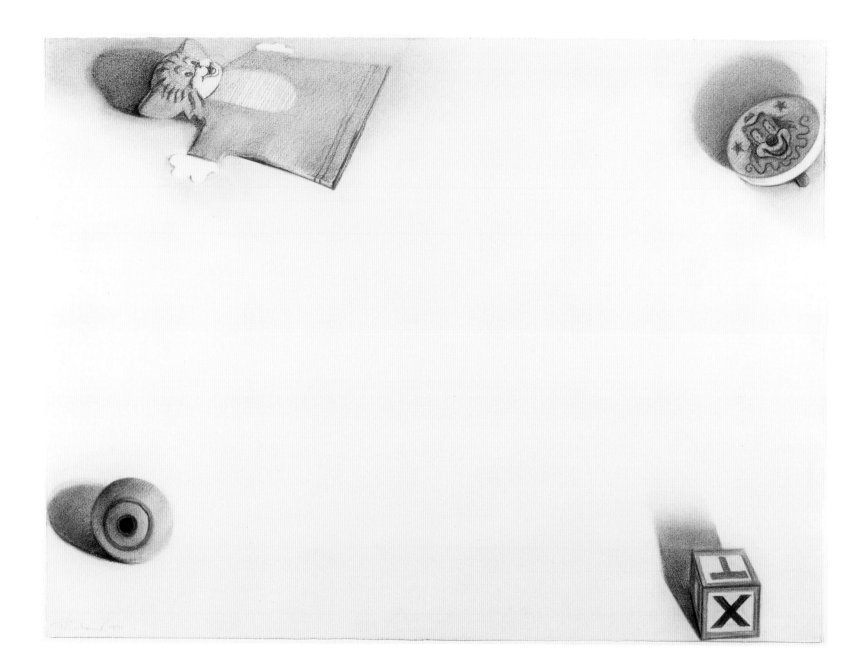

34. *Toys*, 1971. Charcoal on paper, 22¼ x 29¾ in. (sheet). Courtesy of the artist

35. *Pastel Scatter*, 1972. Pastel on paper, 16 x 20⅛ in. (sheet). Courtesy of the Wayne Thiebaud Foundation

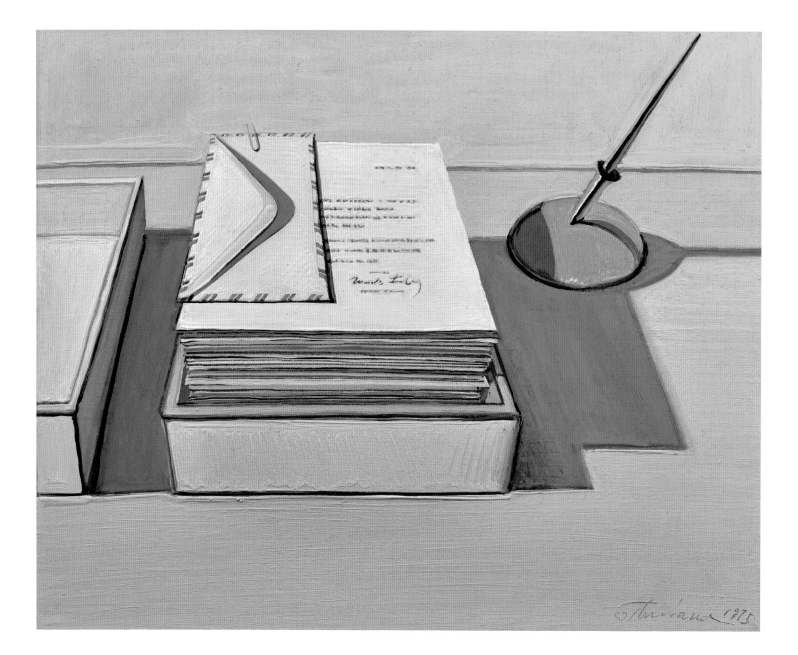

36. *Office Still Life*, 1975. Oil on canvas, 15¾ x 20 in. Courtesy of the artist

37. *Tapestry Skirt*, 1976/1982/1983/2003. Oil on canvas, 42 x 42 in. Courtesy of the Wayne Thiebaud Foundation

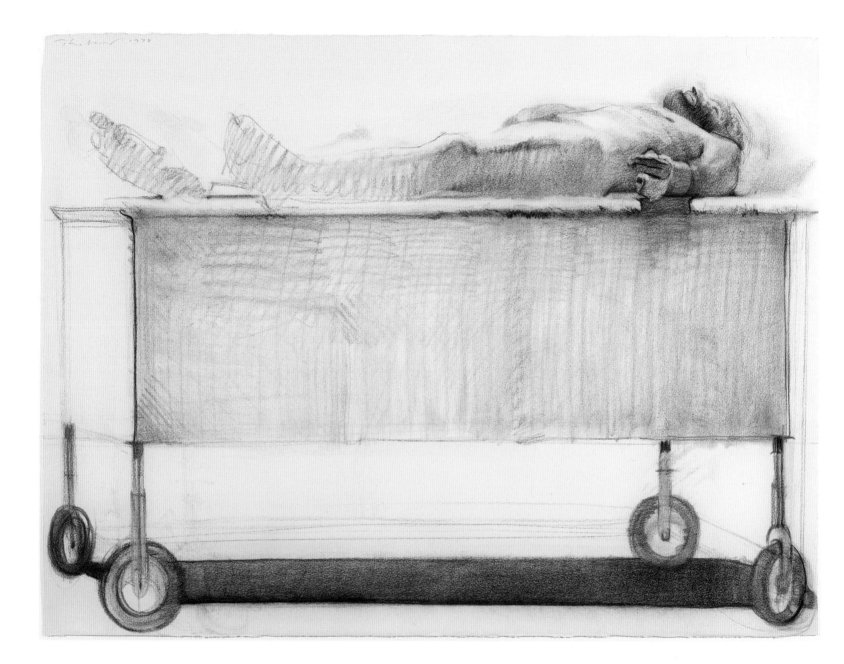

38. *Man on Table*, 1978. Charcoal on paper, 22¼ x 29⅞ in. Collection of Paul LeBaron Thiebaud Trust

39. *Untitled (Van)*, 1979. Monotype with pastel, 11¼ x 13¾ in. (image); 14⅞ x 18⅜ in. (sheet).
Crocker Art Museum, gift of the artist's family, 1995.9.46

40. *Salt Shaker*, 1979. Watercolor and pastel on paper, 7¾ x 7⅞ in. Courtesy of the artist

41. *Untitled (Banana Split)*, c. 1980. Acrylic on paper, 9⅛ x 12¾ in. Collection of Matt and Maria Bult

42. *Virginia Landscape*, 1981. Oil on canvas, 12 x 15⅞ in. Courtesy of the Wayne Thiebaud Foundation

43. *Street and Shadow*, 1982–1983/1996. Oil on linen, 35¾ x 23¾ in. Crocker Art Museum, gift of the artist's family, 1996.3

44. *Untitled (Page of Sketches with Candied Apples and Watermelon Slices)*, early 1980s.
Graphite on paper, 8¼ x 11¼ in. (sheet). Courtesy of the artist

45. *Sardines*, 1982/1990. Etching hand-worked with watercolor, 11¹³⁄₁₆ x 9 in. (plate); 13⅝ x 10⅞ in. (sheet).
Crocker Art Museum, gift of the artist's family, 1995.9.34

46. *Auburn Hills*, 1984. Pastel on paper, 14⅞ x 22⅛ (sheet). Collection of Matt and Maria Bult

47. *Police Car*, 1984. Oil on linen, 16³⁄₁₆ x 16¹⁄₁₆ in. Courtesy of the Wayne Thiebaud Foundation

48. *Untitled (Six Soda Pops)*, c. 1985. Watercolor on paper, 14⅛ x 22⅜ in. Collection of Matt and Maria Bult

49. *Sliced Circle*, 1986. Oil on paper mounted on board, 16⅝ x 22 in. Collection of Paul LeBaron Thiebaud Trust

50. *Apartment Hill*, 1986. Etching hand-worked with pencil, 23¾ x 17½ in. (plate); 29¾ x 22⅜ in. (sheet).
Crocker Art Museum, gift of the artist's family, 1995.9.49

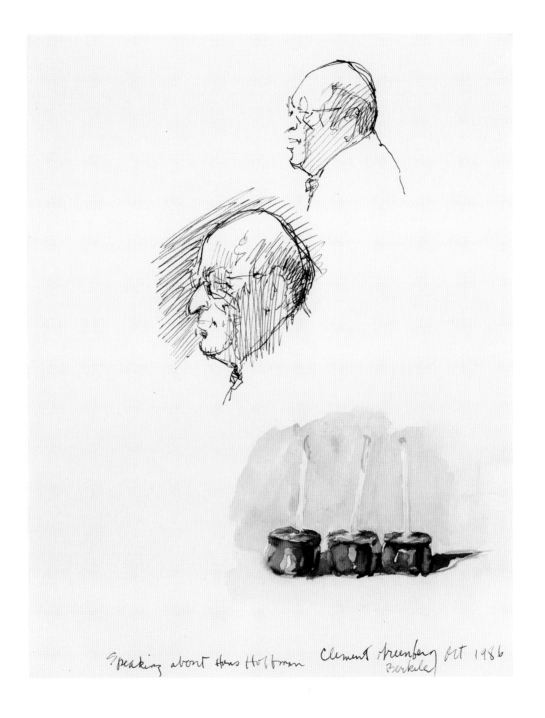

Speaking about Hans Hoffman   *Clement Greenberg Oct 1986 Berkeley*

51. *Untitled (Page of Sketches with Portraits of Clement Greenberg and Candied Apples)*, 1986.
Pen, ink, and watercolor on paper, 11 x 8½ in. (sheet). Courtesy of the artist

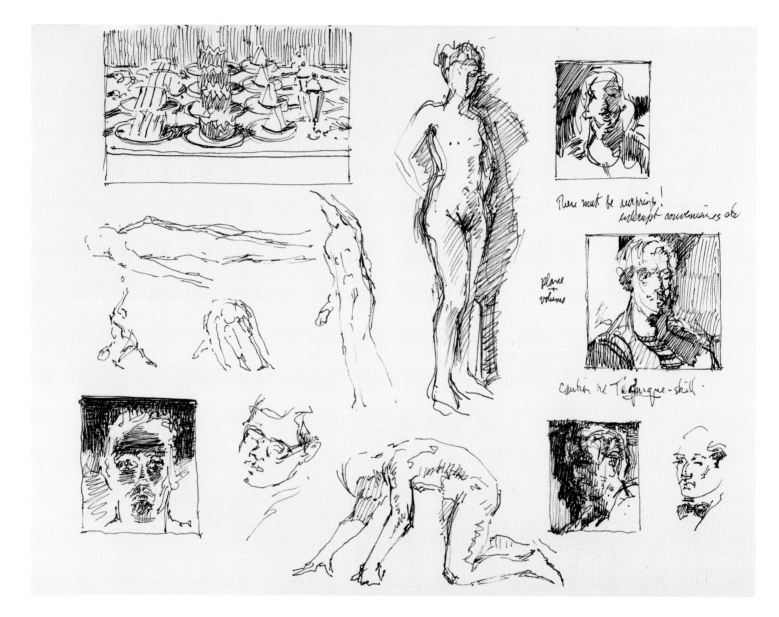

52. *Untitled (Page of Sketches with Figures and Desserts)*, n.d. Ink on paper, 11¼ x 15 in.
Crocker Art Museum, gift of the artist's family, 1995.9.2.a

53. *Untitled (Page of Sketches with Figures and Camels)*, n.d. Ink on paper, 10¾ x 15 in. (sheet).
Crocker Art Museum, gift of the artist's family, 1995.9.8.b

54. *Untitled (Page of Sketches with Figures, Foods, and Seascape)*, n.d.
Ink and watercolor on paper, 10¾ x 8½ in. Crocker Art Museum, gift of the artist's family, 1995.9.11

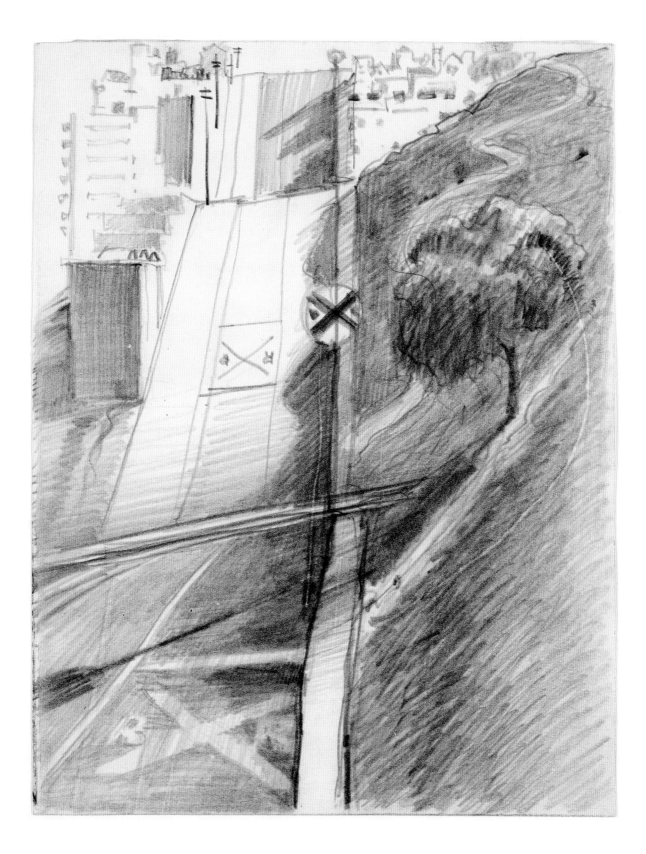

55. *Untitled (Cityscape)*, n.d. Graphite on paper, 11 x 8¾ in. (sheet). Crocker Art Museum, gift of the artist's family, 1995.9.15

56. *Tennis Player (Paul)*, 1987. Oil on canvas, 19 x 23¼ in. Collection of Paul LeBaron Thiebaud Trust

57. *Untitled (Portrait of Matt Bult)*, 1987. Oil on linen, 20 x 23¹³⁄₁₆ in. Collection of Matt and Maria Bult

58. *Violin*, 1987. Charcoal on paper, 15⅛ x 10¹³⁄₁₆ in. Courtesy of the artist

T.P.   Thiebaud 1988

59. *Lipsticks*, 1988. Color etching hand-worked with colored pencil, 6⅞ x 5¹³⁄₁₆ in. (plate); 16 x 14¾ in. (sheet).
Crocker Art Museum, gift of the artist's family, 1995.9.39

60. *Heavy Traffic*, 1988. Oil on paper mounted on board, 14 x 17 in. Courtesy of the Wayne Thiebaud Foundation

61. *Untitled (Study for Office Still Life)*, 1988. Oil on board, 4⅞ x 5⅜ in. Courtesy of the artist

62. *Self-Portrait (4 Hour Study)*, 1989. Oil on board, 11½ x 12 in. Collection of Paul LeBaron Thiebaud Trust

63. *Watermelon and Knife*, 1989. Pastel on paper, 8⅝ x 9⁷⁄₁₆ in. Crocker Art Museum, gift of the artist's family, 1995.9.30

64. *Cow Ridge*, n.d. Etching hand-worked with colored pencil, 8¹⁵⁄₁₆ x 11⅞ in. (plate); 14¹⁵⁄₁₆ x 17¹⁄₁₆ in. (sheet).
Crocker Art Museum, gift of the artist's family, 1995.9.42

Potrero Hill

[signature] 1989.

65. *Potrero Hill*, 1989. Graphite on paper, 10⅜ x 8¹¹⁄₁₆ in. Crocker Art Museum, gift of the artist's family, 1995.9.18.a

66. *Butterfly and Flower*, 1990. Watercolor on paper, 11 x 10¹⁄₁₆ in. Collection of Matt and Maria Bult

67. *Cracker Circle*, 1991. Ink and watercolor on cardstock, 11⁹⁄₁₆ x 9⅜ in. Crocker Art Museum, gift of the artist's family, 1995.9.28

68. *Dark Glasses*, 1991. Gouache on paper, 6⅞ x 11½ in. Crocker Art Museum, gift of the artist's family, 1995.9.29

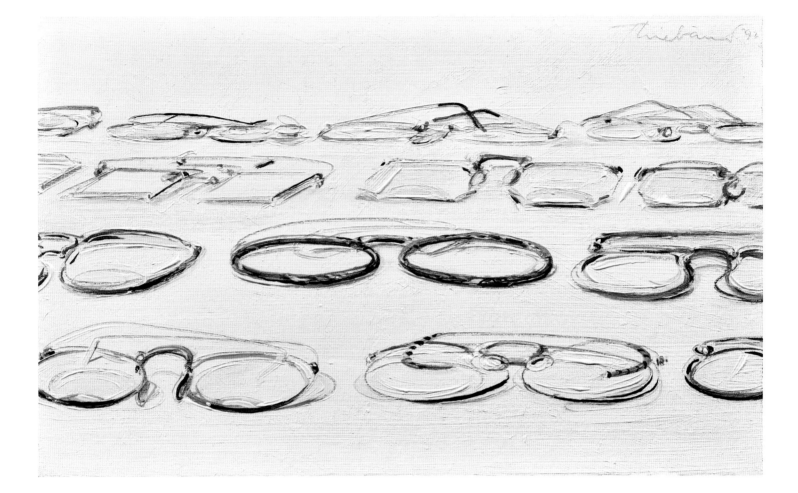

69. *Untitled (Row of Glasses)*, 1992. Oil on board, 7 x 11½ in. Courtesy of the artist

Farm Hill

Thiebaud 1992

70. *Farm Hill*, 1992. Watercolor monotype, 9⅝ x 12⅜ in. (plate); 16⅝ x 18⅞ in. (sheet). Crocker Art Museum, gift of the artist's family, 1995.9.43

71. *Central City*, 1992. Pastel and watercolor on paper, 17½ x 12¼ in. Collection of Matt and Maria Bult

72. *Food Bowls*, 1992/2000/2005. Oil on canvas, 23⅞ x 35⅞ in. Courtesy of the artist

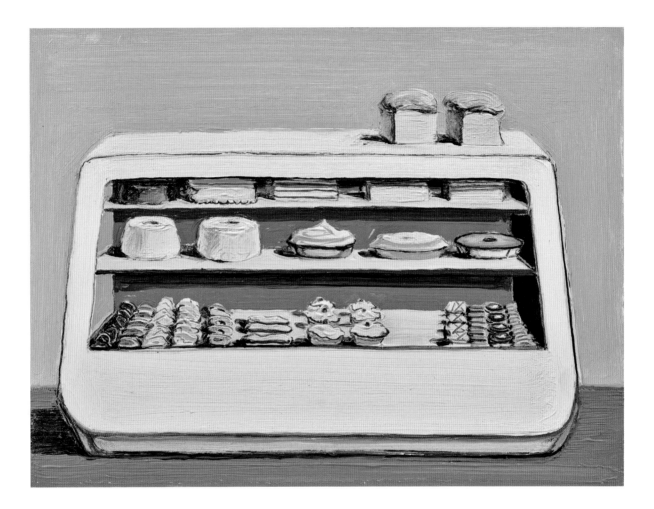

73. *Bakery Counter*, 1993. Oil on graphite on paper, 9⅛ x 12 in. (sheet). Courtesy of the artist

74. *Bow Ties*, 1993. Color lithograph hand-worked with pastel, 9⅞ x 13⅝ in. (image); 15 x 19⅞ in. (sheet).
Crocker Art Museum, gift of the artist's family, 1995.9.38

75. *Dark Chocolates*, n.d. Etching hand-worked with colored pencil, 8⅞ x 10¼ in. (plate); 14⅜ x 15¼ in. (sheet).
Crocker Art Museum, gift of the artist's family, 1995.9.36

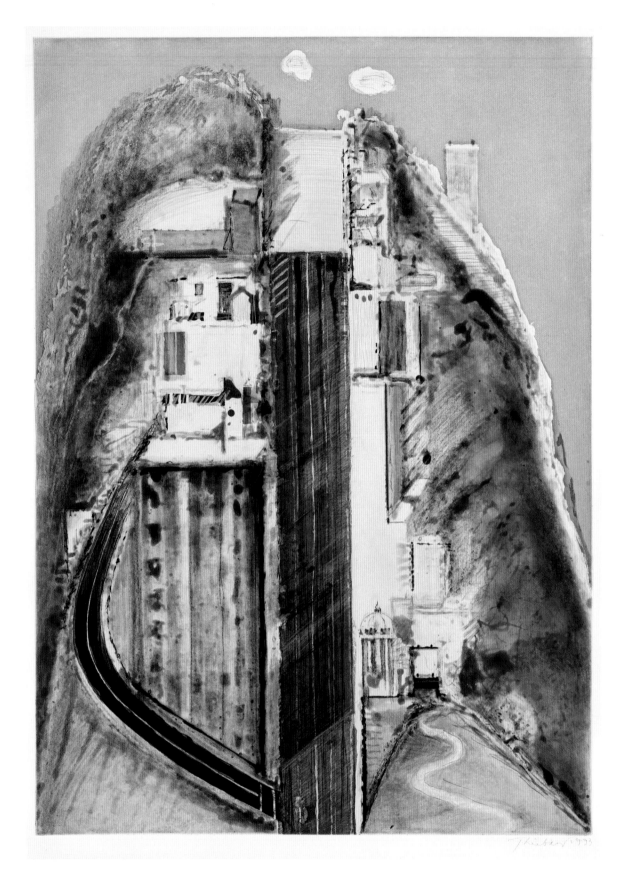

76. *Steep Street*, 1993. Color etching and aquatint hand-worked with waxed crayon, colored pencil, graphite, and gouache, 29⅝ x 21½ in. (plate); 35⅛ x 26⁵⁄₁₆ in. (sheet). Crocker Art Museum, gift of the artist's family, 1995.9.52

77. *Untitled (City View)*, 1993. Oil on canvas, 20 x 16 in. Courtesy of the artist

78. *Valley Farm*, 1993. Softground color etching and aquatint hand-worked with colored pencil, 21½ x 15⅞ in.
(plate); 27¼ x 19¾ in. (sheet). Crocker Art Museum, gift of the artist's family, 1995.9.51

79. *Park Place*, 1995. Color etching hand-worked with watercolor, gouache, colored pencil, graphite, and pastel, 29⁹⁄₁₆ x 20¾ in. (sheet/image). Crocker Art Museum, gift of the artist's family, 1995.9.50

80. *Seven Cupcake Rows*, 1995. Charcoal on paper, 22¾ x 29¾ in. Collection of Paul LeBaron Thiebaud Trust

81. *Untitled (Candied Apples)*, 1998. Oil on board, 6⅛ x 7½ in. Courtesy of the artist

82. *Brown River*, 1998. Oil on canvas, 24 x 28 in. Courtesy of the Wayne Thiebaud Foundation

83. *Y River*, 1998. Oil on canvas, 72 x 72 in. Courtesy of the Wayne Thiebaud Foundation

84. *Hat Rack*, 1999. Oil on board, 14⅛ x 10 in. Courtesy of the artist

85. *Untitled (Rows of Glasses)*, 2000. Oil on linen, 29¹³⁄₁₆ x 23⅞ in. Courtesy of the Wayne Thiebaud Foundation

86. *Jolly Cones*, 2002. Oil on wood, 10¾ x 8 in. Courtesy of the artist

TPA   Thiebaud 02

87. *Toy Box*, 2002. Etching, 16¼ x 12⁹⁄₁₆ in. Courtesy of LeBaron's Fine Art

88. *Stuffed Toys*, 2004. Oil on board, 24 x 22⅛ in. Courtesy of the Wayne Thiebaud Foundation

89. *River Lands (Study)*, 2005. Oil and graphite on paper, 29 x 21¼ in. Courtesy of the artist

90. *River Intersection*, 2010. Oil on canvas, 48 x 36 in. Crocker Art Museum, gift of the Thiebaud Family, 2010.10

91. *Dark Ridge*, 2010/2012/2019. Oil and charcoal on board, 24¼ x 24¼ in. Courtesy of the artist

92. *Palm Tree and Cloud*, 2012. Oil on board, 12⅛ x 9⅞ in. Courtesy of the artist

93. *Clown with Red Hair*, 2015. Oil on board, 12⅛ x 9 in. Private collection

94. *Bumping Clowns*, 2016. Oil on linen, 24 x 36 in. Peress Family Collection

95. *Untitled (Deli)*, 2016. Oil on canvas, 36 x 48 in. Courtesy of the artist

96. *Clown Angel and Dog*, 2017. Oil on board, 29¾ x 24 in. Courtesy of the artist

97. *Clown Boots*, 2018/2019. Oil on canvas, 18 x 18 in. Courtesy of the artist

98. *Yellow Hat*, 2018. Oil on board, 16 x 20 in. Courtesy of the artist

99. *Dress Shoes*, 2018/2019. Oil on canvas, 16 x 20 in. Courtesy of the artist

100. *Sunset Streets Study*, 2019. Oil on board, 14⅛ x 12 in. Courtesy of the artist

CHRONOLOGY

* This chronology draws from Mary Okin's archival research, her interviews with the artist, and the following exhibition catalogues: Gene Cooper, *Wayne Thiebaud: Survey 1947–1976* (1976); Karen Tsujimoto, *Wayne Thiebaud* (1985); Steven A. Nash and Adam Gopnik, *Wayne Thiebaud: A Paintings Retrospective* (2000); Acquavella Galleries, *California Landscapes: Richard Diebenkorn / Wayne Thiebaud* (2018); Rachel Teagle, *Wayne Thiebaud: 1958–1968* (2018); and Isabelle Dervaux, *Wayne Thiebaud: Draftsman* (2018)

1917

Morton J. Thiebaud weds Alice Eugena LeBaron in Phoenix on April 10

1920

Morton Wayne Thiebaud is born in Mesa, Arizona, on November 15; the family calls him Wayne

1921

Thiebaud family moves to Long Beach, California, close to where family members own a farm

1926

Thiebaud's sister Marjory J. Thiebaud is born

1929–1933

Works odd jobs, such as delivering milk, selling newspapers, working as a lifeguard, and working at a hot-dog stand on Rainbow Pier in Long Beach

1930

Morton J. S. Thiebaud is registered as an automotive works manager, and the Thiebaud family lives in Huntington Park, near Los Angeles

1931–1933

Thiebaud family moves to Thorley Ranch, located between St. George and Cedar City in southern Utah, where they raise sheep and agricultural products. The Thiebauds try to own their own farm in southern Utah but are unsuccessful. Leaving the family behind at a hotel in St. George, Utah, Thiebaud's father returns to Long Beach, California, in search of work in the aftermath of the 1933 Long Beach earthquake

1933

Morton J. S. Thiebaud arrives in Long Beach and finds work in construction; the family rejoins him in California. Thiebaud attends public school, plays sports, designs theater sets and posters, joins the Boy Scouts, and participates in activities sponsored by the Mormon church, where his father becomes a bishop

1935–1938

Attends Long Beach Polytechnic High School, where he takes classes in art and art appreciation and continues to develop his talent for drawing

1936

Apprentices for the summer in the animation department at Walt Disney Studios, Los Angeles, where he participates in a labor strike and is fired as a result

1938

Breaks his back playing sports with friends. Graduates from Long Beach Polytechnic High School

1938–1939

Attends Frank Wiggins Trade School, Los Angeles, to study commercial art and sign painting. Apprentices at Sears, Roebuck and Company

1938–1940

Works at various jobs, including as a movie-theater usher and as a freelance cartoonist and illustrator

1940–1941

Studies commercial art at Long Beach Junior College (now Long Beach City College) in Long Beach, California

1942

On September 19, 1942, enlists in the United States Army Air Forces and is assigned to Mather Field in Sacramento. There, he works on the serialized comic strip *Aleck* for the base's newsletter, *Wing Tips*, and designs posters, murals, and other projects

Wayne Thiebaud, c. 1924. Photograph by Hartsook Photo, San Francisco

1943

Marries Patricia Patterson and becomes stepfather to her daughter, Jill

Designs a series of product advertisements for Weinstock, Lubin, and Co., a department-store chain headquartered in Sacramento

Along with other service artists at Mather Field, learns poster-making techniques from inmates at Folsom Prison and sets up a silk-screen printing press at Mather Field

1944

While at Mather Field, continues to produce cartoons and other commercial illustrations

1945

Two works are displayed in the Kingsley Art Club's Twentieth Kingsley Annual exhibition held at the E. B. Crocker Art Gallery (now Crocker Art Museum), Sacramento

Transfers to the First Motion Picture Unit of the United States Army Air Forces in Culver City, California, during his last months of military service, where he helps produce training, morale, and propaganda posters and films. After release from service, moves to New York City and attempts to find work as a professional cartoonist. While there, works in the art department at Fairchild Publications, a publisher of fashion magazines

Returns to California and, after a brief stint in Sacramento, settles in Los Angeles

On December 9, Patricia gives birth to daughter Twinka, their first child together

1946–1949

Works as an art advisor at Universal-International Pictures and does freelance commercial work for Allied Advertising Agency and Rexall Drug Company World Headquarters in Los Angeles. Rexall hires Thiebaud as a layout designer and cartoonist in their advertising department, which publishes his comic strip *Ferbus*. There, he meets Robert Mallary, a young painter and sculptor who becomes an artistic and intellectual mentor and close friend. Mallary encourages Thiebaud to start reading literature and philosophy and to pursue fine-art projects in addition to commercial illustration and layout design, which inspires Thiebaud's decision to leave Rexall Drugs and become a painter and art educator. At Rexall, Thiebaud and Mallary both participate in a labor strike

1948

Thiebaud's work is included in the exhibition *Artists of Los Angeles and Vicinity* at the Museum of History, Science and Art in Los Angeles (now the Los Angeles County Museum of Art)

1949

Thiebaud's paintings are included along with eight other painters in *Artists under Thirty-Three* at the Los Angeles Art Association Galleries, which travels to the San Francisco Museum of Art (now the

San Francisco Museum of Modern Art). Receives a commendation for *Portrait*, a painting of his daughter Twinka. *City Patterns*, an abstract impressionist painting, is also included and awarded second prize in the Twenty-Fourth Kingsley Annual exhibition at the E. B. Crocker Art Gallery. Receives honorable mention for a seascape in oil at the Sarah Singer Memorial Exhibit at the Jewish Institute in Hollywood

Resigns from Rexall Drugs and, under the GI Bill, begins art-education coursework at San José State College (now San José State University), San Jose, California, a teacher-training institution where he studies with Richard Tansey, Marques Reitzel, and others. Plays for the college's tennis team

1950

Moves to Sacramento and continues to pursue a degree in art education at Sacramento State College (now California State University, Sacramento)

Becomes the design and art consultant for the California State Fair in Sacramento, a summer position that will continue for a decade. At the 1950 fair, exhibits a painting titled *The Bell*. Also designs sets for *The Heiress*, a play at the Sacramento State College theater and shows work at the Twenty-Fifth Kingsley Annual exhibition at the E. B. Crocker Art Gallery

Patricia Patterson Thiebaud becomes assistant to Don Birrell, director and curator at the E. B. Crocker Art Gallery

Wayne Thiebaud (back row, second from right) *with Sacramento State College tennis team*, c. 1951. Photographer unknown

1951

First solo museum exhibition, *Influences on a Young Painter—Wayne Thiebaud*, is held at the E. B. Crocker Art Gallery. The exhibition includes sixty pieces in various media and establishes a long tradition of substantive solo exhibitions at the Crocker. Following this exhibition, has another solo exhibition at the Contemporary Gallery in Sausalito, California, and a show titled *Wayne Thiebaud: Prints* at the California State Library in Sacramento, which includes monotypes, silk screens, and lithographs. Also wins first prize for an oil painting titled *Waiting Figures*, which depicts three men at a shoeshine stand, in the Twenty-Sixth Kingsley Annual exhibition at the E. B. Crocker Art Gallery

Completes bachelor of arts degree at Sacramento State College and is hired as an instructor of art at Sacramento Junior College (now Sacramento City College), where he goes on to teach art, art appreciation, art history, filmmaking, television and film production, and commercial design courses

1952

Collaborates with Jerry McLaughlin on *Fountain of Play*, a moving sculpture propelled by water and lit with colored overhead light, part of an open-air art exhibit at the California State Fair. Thiebaud's watercolor painting *Savage Wedding* wins a top prize at the Twenty-Seventh Kingsley Annual exhibition at the E. B. Crocker Art Gallery

Daughter Mallary Ann, named in honor of Robert Mallary, is born on May 11

1953

Wins first prize for his oil painting *The Feast* at the Twenty-Eighth Kingsley Annual exhibition at the E. B. Crocker Art Gallery. Shows work at the Crocker's *Sixth Annual Northern California Arts Exhibition of Graphic and Decorative Arts*, including a study of a head, *Boy*, and a landscape titled *Mistletoe*

Wayne Thiebaud, his first solo show in Los Angeles, is held at the Zivile Gallery. Also shows a series of monotypes at Chouinard Art Institute in Los Angeles

Designs sets for *Madwoman of Chaillot* at the Eaglet Theater in Sacramento

Receives master of arts degree in art from Sacramento State College

1954

Gump's gallery in San Francisco mounts *Paintings: Wayne Thiebaud*, his first solo exhibition in San Francisco, which includes a new series of paintings of public monuments

Is elected chairman of the Sacramento Junior College Art Department faculty and serves in this position until 1956

Exhibits work in the *Third International Biennial of Contemporary Color Lithography* at the Cincinnati Art Museum, Cincinnati

Establishes Patrician Films, through which he produces eleven educational short films about art-making, creativity, and art history. The films are produced in collaboration with Patrick Dullanty, Mel Ramos, and other artists in Thiebaud's circle and distributed by Bailey Films in Hollywood

1955

Shows work at San José State College and the Tivoli Gallery in Hollywood and creates some of his first paintings explicitly focused on food

Patrician Films produces *Space*, a 16 mm educational short that "explains various ways of obtaining space and distance in drawings and paintings"; it wins first prize at the California State Fair

1956

Submits work to the *Fourth International Biennial of Contemporary Color Lithography* at the Cincinnati Art Museum, Cincinnati. Shows work locally at Sacramento State College, Sacramento Junior College, and at Breuners Home Furnishings. At the California State Library, Sacramento, shows two lithographs: *Hansel and Gretel* and *Mother and Daughter*

His film *Space* wins the Chicago Golden Reel Award. Designs sets for *Embarcadero*, a musical about San Francisco staged at Sacramento Junior College

1956–1957

Takes an unpaid sabbatical and moves to New York City. Helps Paul Beckman, chairman of Sacramento State College's art department, recruit art-world figures to meet with Sacramento State College students planning to visit New York and its arts institutions in December. Befriends Willem and Elaine de Kooning, Franz Kline, Barnett Newman, Philip Pearlstein, Milton Resnick, Harold Rosenberg, and other New York artists and critics. Supports himself and his family by working as an art and layout director at Deutsch and Shea Advertising Agency and Frederick A. Richardson Company. Also visits museum collections and, on Friday nights, attends lectures, panel discussions, and social gatherings at the Eighth Street Club and Cedar Tavern

1957

Returns to Sacramento

Expressionistic figure drawings that illustrate "social problems" are shown at Sacramento Junior College and in the lobby of the Sacramento State College theater, the latter displayed in conjunction with the college's production of *Death of a Salesman*

Work painted in New York that evidences the influence of Abstract Expressionism is exhibited at the E. B. Crocker Art Gallery in *Seven Artists under Thirty*, a show that includes six other painters who also attended Sacramento State College. The Prints Room of the California State Library in Sacramento hosts *Twelve Years of Drawings by Wayne Thiebaud*. Holds solo exhibition *Thiebaud—Recent Works* at the E. B. Crocker Art Gallery, many of the oils and watercolors featuring New York scenes

Wins the Osborn Cunningham prize for watercolors at the San Francisco Museum of Art. Is selected by architects of the firm Dreyfuss and Blackford to design a mosaic mural for the exterior of the Sacramento Municipal Utility District (SMUD) headquarters building, which results in *Water City*. Wins a purchase award at the Sacramento State Fair for his silkscreen print *Bridge City*

1958

Water City mosaic arrives from Italy and is installed on the exterior of the SMUD headquarters building in Sacramento. He is nominated for the 1959 Ford Foundation Award for the Visual Arts

Cofounds the Artists Cooperative Gallery (ACG, later Artists Contemporary Gallery) in Sacramento with Patrick Dullanty, Eben Jordan Haskell, Gregory Kondos, Jack Ogden, and Mel Ramos, as well as entrepreneur Russ Solomon

Artists Wayne Thiebaud, Mel Ramos, Jack Ogden, Don Nice, and Gregory Kondos (left to right), mid-1970s. Photographer unknown

The ACG hosts *Recent Works of Wayne Thiebaud*. Exhibits work in the *Fifth International Biennial of Contemporary Color Lithography* at the Cincinnati Art Museum, Cincinnati

Serves as guest instructor (substituting for Nathan Oliveira) at the California School of Fine Arts (now the San Francisco Art Institute), San Francisco. Is re-elected department chairman at Sacramento Junior College. Wins a national Columbia Records painting contest inspired by Dave Brubeck's new album *Jazz Impressions of Eurasia*

Work is included in the *Sacramento Artists' League Exhibition* at the E. B. Crocker Art Gallery, the *Northern California Artists' Open*, and the Thirty-Third Kingsley Annual exhibition. Also has work in the *San Francisco Art Association Annual Print and Drawing Exhibition*

After fifteen years of marriage, Wayne and Patricia Thiebaud divorce

1959

Wayne Thiebaud – Recent Works opens at the ACG in Sacramento. Work is selected for the San Francisco Art Association's *Seventy-Eighth Annual Painting and Sculpture Exhibition* at the San Francisco Museum of Art. Is voted an artist member of the San Francisco Art Association

Marries Betty Jean Carr on December 11 and becomes stepfather to her son, Matthew Bult. On their honeymoon, the couple travels to Mexico with their family. Thiebaud paints *Beach Boys* and other beach scenes with palm trees and food stands. Photographs food displays on the trip

1960

Richard L. Nelson, founder of the recently assembled art department at the University of California, Davis, recruits Thiebaud to join the faculty. In commenting on Thiebaud's resignation, the President of Sacramento Junior College states, "We are sorry indeed to lose such a valuable faculty member. . . . The many prizes and awards won by his students are the best testimony to his ability as an outstanding and inspiring teacher."

Holds solo exhibition *Paintings by Wayne Thiebaud* at the Nut Tree in Vacaville, California. *Wayne Thiebaud* is shown at the Humboldt State College (now Humboldt State University) art gallery in Arcata,

California, and at the ACG, Sacramento. Other works are included in exhibitions at the San Francisco Museum of Art; at the Staempfli Gallery, New York; and at the Tanager Gallery, New York. Is included in the Thirty-Fifth Kingsley Annual exhibition at the E. B. Crocker Art Gallery. Wins "best of show" at the Sacramento County Fair for *Beach Boys*

Son Paul LeBaron Thiebaud is born on October 10

1961

Wins honorable mention at the Annual Art Invitational at the Palace of the Legion of Honor in San Francisco for *Beach Boys*. Wins first prize in the Thirty-Sixth Kingsley Annual exhibition for his watercolor *Vendor* and places second in the oil division for the painting *Girl*. Also wins first prize for *Vendor* at the first annual Spring Art Show sponsored by the Lodi Community Arts Center. The ACG hosts *Wayne Thiebaud*, a show that includes food paintings. Art Unlimited Gallery holds the first San Francisco exhibition of Thiebaud's food paintings, *An Exhibition of Recent Works*, which generates no sales

At UC Davis, receives a University of California faculty fellowship and uses the funds to travel that summer to secure gallery representation in New York. After numerous rejections, visits Allan Stone, who, with hesitation, agrees to include Thiebaud's work in an upcoming group exhibition and to host a solo show the following spring

1962

Wayne Thiebaud: Recent Paintings, the first solo exhibition of Thiebaud's work in New York, opens at Allan Stone Gallery in April. The show sells out and receives critical acclaim. *An Exhibition of Paintings by Wayne Thiebaud* subsequently opens at the M. H. de Young Memorial Museum in San Francisco, which then travels to the E. B. Crocker Art Gallery, Sacramento. Late that September, his work is included in *New Painting of Common Objects* at the Pasadena Art Museum (now the Norton Simon Museum), Pasadena, California, and in *International Exhibition of the New Realists* at Sidney Janis Gallery, New York. Work is also included in *Fifty California Artists*, held at the Whitney Museum of American Art, New York

Wayne Thiebaud and wife Betty Jean Thiebaud in New York, early 1960s. Photographer unknown

1963

Begins long association with Kathan Brown, proprietor of Crown Point Press in Oakland (later in San Francisco), California

Travels for the first time to Europe for the opening of *Wayne Thiebaud*, organized by Allan Stone Gallery and shown at the Galleria Schwartz in Milan, the first exhibition of Thiebaud's work in Europe. Allan Stone Gallery also hosts *Wayne Thiebaud*, a solo exhibition of recent work. The Los Angeles County Museum of Art hosts *Six More*, an exhibition of West Coast painting curated by Lawrence Alloway. Work is included in John Coplans's *Pop Art U.S.A.* at the California College of Arts and Crafts (now the California College of the Arts) in Oakland, California, and the Oakland Art Gallery (now the Oakland Museum of California), as well as in *Pop Goes the Easel!* at the Contemporary Arts Association (now the Contemporary Arts Museum), Houston

Is promoted to Associate Professor at UC Davis

1964

Receives grant from the University of California Research Institute and begins a concentrated study of the human figure. Spends extensive time engaged in life drawing, asking friends and family to pose for him

Thiebaud is shown at Allan Stone Gallery. Work is included in the *Thirty-Ninth Annual Exhibition: Work of Artists of Northern California* at the E. B. Crocker Art Gallery. Also has work in *Nieuwe Realisten* at the Gemeentemuseum Den Haag, The Hague, the Netherlands, an exhibition that traveled to 20er Haus (now 21er Haus), Vienna, as *Pop Etc.* and to Akademie der Künste, Berlin, as *Realisten und Pop Art*

1965

The E. B. Crocker Art Gallery hosts its first annual *Crocker Art Gallery Association Invitational*, to which Thiebaud submits *Man in Blue Chair*. Work is also included in the E. B. Crocker Art Gallery's *West Coast Watercolor Society Invitational* and in two traveling group exhibitions on the East Coast, *The Figure International* and *Modern Realism and Surrealism*. The Stanford Art Museum at Stanford University (now the Iris and B. Gerald Cantor Center for Visual Arts) opens *Figures: Thiebaud*, the artist's first exhibition of life-sized figure paintings. The exhibition travels to Allan Stone Gallery and the Albrecht Gallery (now the Albrecht-Kemper Museum of Art) in St. Joseph, Missouri. Exhibits print series *Delights* at the E. B. Crocker Art Gallery. The San Francisco Museum of Art mounts *Prints, Drawings, and Paintings by Wayne Thiebaud*

1966

Wayne Thiebaud: Paintings, Drawings, Prints, and Watercolors opens at the art gallery at Humboldt State College in Arcata, California. Work is included in *American Masters: 150 Years of American Paintings from California Museums* at the Santa Barbara Museum of Art, Santa Barbara, California, which travels to the E. B. Crocker Art Gallery. Group shows include: *The Current Moment in Art* at the San Francisco Museum of Art and the San Francisco Art Institute; *The Harry N. Abrams Collection* at the Jewish Museum, New York; *The Second Bucknell Annual Drawing Exhibition*, Bucknell University Art Gallery,

Artists Gregory Kondos and Wayne Thiebaud painting outside Wayne's 5th Avenue residence, Sacramento, c. 1965. Photograph by Betty Jean Thiebaud

Lewisburg, Pennsylvania; and *Sculpture and Painting Today* at the Museum of Fine Arts, Boston

The April cover of *ARTnews* features *Girl in White Boots*, one of the paintings traveling as part of *Figures: Thiebaud*

1967

Allan Stone Gallery opens *Wayne Thiebaud*, an exhibition of recent work. Stone facilitates Thiebaud's inclusion in *Environments USA 1957–1967*, the United States exhibition at the São Paulo Art Biennial. Work is included in the ACG's *The Organizers, 10th Year*, a group exhibition celebrating the gallery's ten-year anniversary

Is promoted to full professor at UC Davis and also serves as a visiting professor of art and an artist-in-residence at Cornell University, Ithaca, New York. Moves with his family to Rosebud Ranch (or Rosebud Farm), an 1877 farm complex built by pioneer architect Nathaniel Goodell (who also designed California's Governor's mansion). Located on the Sacramento River south of Sacramento in Hood, California, the picturesque building and grounds were featured in Betty Jean Thiebaud's film *Wayne Thiebaud* (1971). After Thiebaud sells the property, and in part because of his residency there, the ranch becomes a National Historic Landmark in 1979

1968

The retrospective *Wayne Thiebaud: Artist in Mid Career* is organized by John Coplans at the Pasadena Art Museum, Pasadena, California. The exhibition travels to the Walker Art Center in Minneapolis; the San Francisco Museum of Art; the Contemporary Arts Center in Cincinnati; and the Utah Museum of Fine Arts in Salt Lake City. Allan Stone Gallery hosts *Wayne Thiebaud*, an exhibition of recent work. The exhibition *Thiebaud* is held at the Milwaukee Art Center (now the Milwaukee Art Museum)

Receives a commission from *Sports Illustrated* to travel to London and create four paintings of the Wimbledon tennis tournament, which are reproduced in the June 24, 1968, issue

Completes a limited edition of lithographs titled *Suckers State I* and *Suckers State II* at Gemini GEL, a Los Angeles artists' workshop and publisher of limited edition fine-art prints and sculptures

1969

Exhibition *Recent Works of Wayne Thiebaud* is held at Allan Stone Gallery. Work is included in the exhibition *Kompas 4: West Coast USA* at the Stedelijk van Abbe Museum in Eindhoven, the Netherlands. Also included in *American Art: The 1960s*, a traveling exhibition organized by the Georgia Museum of Art, University of Georgia, Athens

In the summer, teaches at the New York Studio School in Paris with Elaine de Kooning. Also helps establish the visiting artist program at UC Davis; invited artists include Robert Mallary, Joseph Raffael, Elaine de Kooning, Richard Artschwager, Robert Frank, John Cage, and William Wegman

1970

E. B. Crocker Art Gallery mounts *Recent Works by Wayne Thiebaud*. Allan Stone Gallery mounts *Wayne Thiebaud: Recent Works*. Fresno State College Art Gallery in Fresno, California, hosts *Wayne Thiebaud*. Work is included in the group show *A Century of California Painting: 1870–1970* organized by the Crocker Citizens Plaza (now 611 Place),

Alice Eugena "Jean" Thiebaud and son Wayne Thiebaud at his San Francisco home, mid-1970s. Photograph by Betty Jean Thiebaud

Los Angeles, which travels to the Fresno Art Center, Fresno, California; the California Palace of the Legion of Honor, San Francisco; the de Saisset Museum at the University of Santa Clara (now Santa Clara University), Santa Clara, California; the E. B. Crocker Art Gallery; and The Oakland Museum, Oakland (now Oakland Museum of California)

Serves as a visiting professor at the University of Victoria in British Columbia, Canada. Works on a series of linocuts through Arnéra printshop in Vallauris, France

1971

Begins to paint San Francisco cityscapes and a series of tabletop compositions of pastel scatters, tools, and desk sets

Berggruen Gallery, San Francisco, exhibits *Wayne Thiebaud: Paintings, Pastels, Drawings, and Prints*. The ACG hosts *Wayne Thiebaud—Delights*. Work is included in the group show *Collectors* at the E. B. Crocker Art Gallery

Betty Jean Thiebaud finishes *Wayne Thiebaud*, a twenty-two-minute documentary film showing her husband's process and ascent in the art world

1971–1976

Two portfolios of prints, *Seven Still Lifes and a Rabbit* and *Seven Still Lifes and a Silver Landscape* are published by Parasol Press Limited in New York, which also organizes the exhibition *Wayne Thiebaud Graphics: 1964–1971*, shown at the Whitney Museum of American Art, New York. In 1972, the exhibition travels to the William Rockhill Nelson Gallery and Atkins Museum of Fine Arts (now the Nelson-Atkins Museum of Art), Kansas City, Missouri; the Corcoran Gallery of Art, Washington, DC; the Achenbach Foundation for Graphic Arts at the California Palace of the Legion of Honor, San Francisco; Fort Wayne Museum of Art, Fort Wayne, Indiana; the Fort Worth Art Museum-Center (now the Modern Art Museum of Fort Worth), Fort Worth, Texas; the Des Moines Art Center, Des Moines, Iowa; the Wadsworth Atheneum, Hartford, Connecticut; the Baltimore Museum of Art, Baltimore; and, in 1973, to the Phoenix Art Museum, Phoenix. In 1975, it travels to the Wallraf-Richartz Museum, Cologne, West Germany; in 1976 to the Arnolfini Gallery, Bristol, England; and, in 1979, to Bard College, Annandale-on-Hudson, New York

1972

Celebrating ten years of collaboration, *Wayne Thiebaud* opens at Allan Stone Gallery. *Wayne Thiebaud: Survey of Painting 1950–1972* is held at the California State University Art Galleries in Long Beach

Is appointed the thirty-first Faculty Research Lecturer at UC Davis and is honored with the Golden Apple Award for distinguished teaching. Earns an honorary doctorate from the California College of Arts and Crafts, Oakland, California

Work is included in *Documenta 5: Inquiry into Reality – Today's Imagery* in Kassel, Germany

Establishes a second home on Potrero Hill in San Francisco, where he further develops cityscape subjects

Artists Chuck Close and Wayne Thiebaud at Allan Stone Gallery, New York, c. 1975. Photograph by Betty Jean Thiebaud

1973

Wayne Thiebaud: Recent Paintings opens at the ACG in Sacramento. The Portland Center for the Visual Arts in Portland, Oregon, opens the retrospective *Wayne Thiebaud: Paintings and Drawings, 1958–1973*. Exhibitions include: *Wayne Thiebaud: Recent Work* at the Allan Stone Gallery; *Wayne Thiebaud: Recent Paintings, Pastels, and Prints* at the Berggruen Gallery, San Francisco; *Works by Wayne Thiebaud* at the South Teaching Gallery (now the Miami Dade College Centre Gallery) of Miami-Dade Community College (now Miami Dade College), Miami, Florida. *Works on Paper and Other Edibles: An Exhibition of the Works of Wayne Thiebaud* also opens at the Holland Union Gallery at Dickinson College in Carlisle, Pennsylvania. Work is included in *Sacramento Sampler II* at the E. B. Crocker Art Gallery

1974

Serves as a visiting professor at Rice University in Houston

Thiebaud in Dakota opens at the University Art Gallery at the University of North Dakota in Grand Forks, North Dakota. *Paintings and Graphics by Wayne Thiebaud* is held at the Gilmore Art Center at the Kalamazoo Institute of Arts, Kalamazoo, Michigan. *Wayne Thiebaud: Paintings, Drawings, and Prints* is shown at Sheppard Fine Arts Gallery (now the John and Geraldine Lilley Museum of Art), University of Nevada, Reno. Work is included in *1974 Kingsley Art Club Open* at the E. B. Crocker Art Gallery

1975

The Edwin A. Ulrich Museum of Art at Wichita State University in Wichita, Kansas, opens *Wayne Thiebaud*, a smaller retrospective exhibition. Work is included in *Fifty Years of Crocker-Kingsley* at the E. B. Crocker Art Gallery

Serves as a visiting professor at Colorado State University in Fort Collins, Colorado, which hosts *Wayne Thiebaud: Prints, Drawings, Paintings*; the exhibition later travels to the Denver Art Museum, Denver

1976

Wayne Thiebaud: Survey, 1947–1976 is organized by the Phoenix Art Museum, Phoenix, and travels to The Oakland Museum, Oakland, California; the University of Southern California in Los Angeles; the Des Moines Art Center, Des Moines, Iowa; Neuberger Museum of Art at Purchase College, State University of New York, Harrison, New York; and the Institute of Contemporary Art, Boston. The accompanying catalogue by Gene Cooper becomes the first definitive source on Thiebaud's career

Wayne Thiebaud opens at the Allan Stone Gallery and *Wayne Thiebaud: Paintings and Works on Paper* opens at the Mary Porter Sesnon Art Gallery at the University of California, Santa Cruz. Work is also included in the group exhibitions *30 Years of American Printmaking* at the Brooklyn Museum, Brooklyn, New York, and *American Master Drawings and Watercolors: Works of Art on Paper from Colonial Times to the Present*, a traveling exhibition organized by the Minneapolis Institute of Arts, Minneapolis

Begins weekly drawing sessions in San Francisco with a group of Bay Area artists, including Mark Adams, William Theophilus Brown, Gordon Cook, and Beth Van Hoesen

Serves as a visiting professor at the University of Utah, Salt Lake City

Betty Jean Thiebaud finishes her best-known documentary film, *Elaine de Kooning Paints a Portrait*

Life drawing class in San Francisco with artists Mark Adams, Beth Van Hoesen, Wayne Thiebaud, William Theophilus Brown, and Gordon Cook (left to right), n.d. Photograph by Diana Crane

1976–1978

The United States Department of the Interior commissions painting *Yosemite Ridge Line* for *America 1976 – A Bicentennial Exhibition*. The exhibition featured commissioned work by forty-four other contemporary artists and traveled to the Corcoran Gallery of Art, Washington, DC (1976); Wadsworth Atheneum, Hartford, Connecticut (1976); Fogg Art Museum, Harvard University, Cambridge, Massachusetts (1976); the Institute of Contemporary Art, Boston (1976); Minneapolis Institute of Arts, Minneapolis (1977); Milwaukee Art Center, Milwaukee (1977); Fort Worth Art Museum, Fort Worth, Texas (1977); San Francisco Museum of Modern Art (1977); High Museum of Art, Atlanta (1977–1978); and the Brooklyn Museum, Brooklyn, New York (1978)

1977

Berggruen Gallery, San Francisco, opens *Wayne Thiebaud: Delights*. *Wayne Thiebaud: Drawings* opens at the Memorial Union Art Gallery at UC Davis. The Visual Arts Gallery (now The Catherine G. Murphy Gallery) at the College of St. Catherine (now St. Catherine University) in St. Paul, Minnesota, hosts *Wayne Thiebaud: Creations on Paper*. The Delphian School in Sheridan, Oregon, hosts *Wayne Thiebaud / Strictly Personal*. Diablo Valley Junior College in Pleasant Hill, California, exhibits *Wayne Thiebaud: Recent Paintings and Drawings*. Work is also included in the exhibition *Representations of America* at the Alexander Pushkin Museum in Moscow, which traveled to The State Hermitage Museum, St. Petersburg, Russia, and the Palace of Art in Minsk, Belarus. Is included in *Artists' Postcards*, a traveling exhibition organized by the Cooper Hewitt, Smithsonian Design Museum, New York

Serves as visiting professor at Stanford University, Stanford, California, where he creates a series of monotypes in collaboration with Nathan Oliveira

Wayne Thiebaud at Crown Point Press, Oakland, 1979. Photograph by Patrick Dullanty

1978

Serves on the Prix de Rome award panel for painting in Rome

Serves as a visiting professor at the Skowhegan School of Painting and Sculpture in Madison, Maine

The Yarlow/Salzman Gallery in Toronto mounts *Wayne Thiebaud: Delights*. The San Francisco Museum of Modern Art opens *Wayne Thiebaud: Recent Work*, featuring Thiebaud's recent cityscapes. *Wayne Thiebaud: Works on Paper* is held at Boise Gallery of Art (now Boise Art Museum), Boise, Idaho. *Wayne Thiebaud* opens at the Boehm Gallery at Palomar College in San Marcos, California. Is included in *Things Seen*, a traveling group exhibition organized by the Sheldon Memorial Art Gallery (now Sheldon Museum of Art), Lincoln, Nebraska

1979

Produces his first cityscape etchings with Crown Point Press in Oakland, California. Allan Stone Gallery exhibits cityscapes in *Wayne Thiebaud: San Francisco Paintings*

1980

Exhibitions include: *Thiebaud* at Allan Stone Gallery; *Wayne Thiebaud: Paintings, Pastels, and Prints*, Berggruen Gallery, San Francisco; *Wayne Thiebaud*, Van Staveren Fine Art, Sacramento, California; *Wayne Thiebaud*, Art Center College of Design, Pasadena, California; *Wayne Thiebaud: Etchings and Serigraphs*, University Union Gallery, California State University, Sacramento; *Wayne Thiebaud: Paintings and Drawings*, Charles Campbell Gallery, San Francisco; and *Wayne Thiebaud*, gallery of the College of the Mainland, Texas City, Texas. Is included in *Still Life Today*, a traveling group exhibition organized by the Goddard Riverside Community Center, New York

1981

Wayne Thiebaud: Painting is organized at the Walker Art Center in Minneapolis and travels to the Fort Worth Art Museum, Fort Worth, Texas; Museum of Fine Arts, St. Petersburg, Florida; and the Institute of Contemporary Art at the University of Pennsylvania, Philadelphia. Smaller exhibitions of paintings and prints are mounted: *Paintings and Prints by Wayne Thiebaud*, Robert Mondavi Winery in Oakville, California; *Wayne Thiebaud: Works on Paper*, California State University, Stanislaus, in Turlock, California; *Prints and Paintings by Wayne Thiebaud*, Marsh Art Gallery at the University of Richmond in Virginia. Work is also included in the Whitney Museum of American Art's Biennial Exhibition and in *Contemporary American Realism*, a traveling group show organized by the Pennsylvania Academy of the Fine Arts, Philadelphia, as well *Real, Really Real, and Super Real*, a traveling group exhibition organized by the San Antonio Museum of Art, San Antonio

Is awarded a Distinguished Teaching of Art award by the College Art Association of America. Serves as a visiting professor at the Laguna Beach School of Art (now the Laguna College of Art and Design), Laguna Beach, California

Designs a lithographic poster for the Los Angeles Bicentennial featuring *Freeways*

1982

Wayne Thiebaud: Recent Drawings is held at the Eloise Pickard Smith Gallery at the University of California, Santa Cruz, and *Wayne Thiebaud* is mounted at the Art Museum of Santa Cruz County (now the Santa Cruz Museum of Art & History), Santa Cruz, California. *Thiebaud Graphics* is held at the Sheehan Gallery at Whitman College in Walla Walla, Washington. Allan Stone Gallery exhibits *Wayne Thiebaud: Recent Paintings*. Davis Art Center (now Davis Arts Center) in Davis, California, presents *Wayne Thiebaud Prints*. *Wayne Thiebaud Prints* opens at Gallery Hiro in Tokyo and travels to the Yoh Art Gallery in Osaka, Japan

1983

The Crocker Art Museum exhibits *Wayne Thiebaud: Landscapes and City Views* and includes Thiebaud's work in *Twenty-Five Years of the Artists Contemporary Gallery*. The Trout Gallery at the Emil R. Weiss Center for the Arts at Dickinson College in Carlisle, Pennsylvania, mounts *Wayne Thiebaud: Paintings, Drawings, Graphics 1961–1983*. Thiebaud receives an honorary doctorate at Dickinson College. Work is included in *West Coast Realism*, a traveling group exhibition organized by the Laguna Beach Museum of Art (now the Laguna Art Museum), Laguna Beach, California

Travels to Kyoto, Japan, to learn *ukiyo-e* printmaking techniques through Crown Point Press's new Japanese Woodblock Program and creates *Dark Cake*, a collaboration with Japanese woodblock printer Tadashi Toda at the Shi-un-do Print Shop in Kyoto

1984

Is awarded the Faculty Research Lecture Medal in conjunction with the fiftieth anniversary of UC Davis. Also receives special recognition from the National Association of Schools of Art and Design and serves as a visiting professor at the New York Studio School of Drawing, Painting, and Sculpture in New York City

Wayne Thiebaud is shown at Davidson Galleries, Seattle, and *Wayne Thiebaud: Drawings* is mounted at the Jeremy Stone Gallery, San Francisco

Wayne Thiebaud with sons Matt Bult (center) *and Paul LeBaron Thiebaud* (right) *at Mary Jensen Gallery, Sacramento*, c. 1985. Photograph by Leta Ramos

Wayne Thiebaud with daughters Twinka Thiebaud (left) *and Mallary Thiebaud* (right), 1985. Photograph by Bruce Forrester

1985

The San Francisco Museum of Modern Art celebrates its fiftieth anniversary with *Wayne Thiebaud*, a retrospective that travels to the Newport Harbor Art Museum (now the Orange County Museum of Art), Newport Beach, California; Milwaukee Art Museum, Milwaukee; the Columbus Museum of Art, Columbus, Ohio; and The Nelson-Atkins Museum of Art, Kansas City, Missouri. The accompanying catalogue by Karen Tsujimoto remains a definitive source on Thiebaud's life and work. *Wayne Thiebaud* is shown at Van Staveren Fine Art in Sacramento

Is elected to the American Academy of Arts and Letters in New York City

Contributes illustrations to *Chez Panisse Desserts*, a book by Lindsey Remolif Shere, pastry chef at Alice Waters's restaurant Chez Panisse in Berkeley, California

1986

Wayne Thiebaud: 25th Anniversary Exhibition is held at Allan Stone Gallery, celebrating the twenty-five-year relationship between Thiebaud and Stone

Is elected Associate National Academician of the National Academy of Design in New York, one of the oldest and most distinguished organizations of artists in the United States

1987

The Arts Club of Chicago exhibits *Wayne Thiebaud: Works on Paper from the Collection of the Artist*, which also travels to the Georgia State University Art Gallery (now the Ernest G. Welch Gallery), Atlanta. Work is also included in *Made in the U.S.A.: An Americanization in Modern Art, the '50s and '60s*, a traveling group exhibition organized by the University Art Museum at the University of California, Berkeley (now the Berkeley Art Museum and Pacific Film Archive). Has work included in *The Artists of California: A Group Portrait in Mixed Media* at The Oakland Museum, Oakland, California, which travels to the Crocker Art Museum, Sacramento, and the Laguna Art Museum, Laguna Beach, California

Receives multiple awards, including the Award of Honor for Distinguished Service to the Arts by the San Francisco Arts Commission; the Cyril Magnin Award for Outstanding Individual Achievement in the Arts on behalf of the San Francisco Chamber of

Commerce. Is inducted into the American Academy of Achievement, Washington, DC. Becomes a full Academician at the National Academy of Design

In collaboration with Tadashi Toda at Shi-un-do Print Shop in Kyoto, Japan, creates two more prints using *ukiyo-e* techniques: *Hill Street* and *Candied Apples*

1988

Exhibition of prints is shown at the Rutgers Barclay Gallery in Santa Fe, New Mexico, and at the Charles Campbell Gallery in San Francisco. *Wayne Thiebaud* is held at Allan Stone Gallery

Receives the UC Davis Prize for Teaching and Scholarly Achievement; is elected a fellow of the Academy of Arts and Sciences in Boston; and is awarded an honorary doctorate by the San Francisco Art Institute

1988–1990

The Richard L. Nelson Gallery at UC Davis organizes *Wayne Thiebaud: Works on Paper, 1947–1987*, which travels to the Stanford University Museum of Art, Stanford, California (1988); Northern Arizona University Art Gallery (now the Northern Arizona University Art Museum), Flagstaff, Arizona (1988); Sweeney Art Gallery, University of California, Riverside (1989); Fresno Art Museum, Fresno, California (1989); Museum of Art (now the Fred Jones Jr. Museum of Art), University of Oklahoma, Norman, Oklahoma (1989); Fine Arts Gallery (now

University Art Gallery), University of California, Irvine (1989); Marjorie Barrick Museum of Art, University of Nevada, Las Vegas (1990)

1989

Wayne Thiebaud: Works on Paper is exhibited at the Mead Art Museum, Amherst College, Amherst, Massachusetts. The Marilyn Butler Gallery in Santa Monica, California, mounts *Wayne Thiebaud*

Creates one of his first "ballroom couple" compositions in drypoint, which leads to a series of paintings on the theme

1990

The Hearst Art Gallery (now the Saint Mary's College Museum of Art) at Saint Mary's College in Moraga, California, exhibits *Thiebaud at Seventy: A Retrospective Selection of Paintings, Drawings, Watercolors, and Prints*. Karsten Schubert Limited in London exhibits *Wayne Thiebaud: Prints and Hand-Coloured Etchings*; Rutgers Barclay Gallery in Santa Fe, New Mexico, hosts *Wayne Thiebaud: Sketchbook Selections*. Work is also included in *Still Life into Object*, a group show at the Museum of Modern Art in New York

Creates *Paint Cans*, a poster for the art exhibition at the Chicago International Art Exposition

Designs set and costumes for *Krazy Kat*, a production by the San Francisco Ballet based on the comic strip illustrated by George Herriman, Thiebaud's favorite cartoonist

After thirty years, retires from full-time faculty position at UC Davis but continues teaching occasional courses as part-time professor emeritus. Receives the Distinguished Service Award from his alma mater, California State University, Sacramento

Paul Thiebaud partners with Charles Campbell, owner of the Charles Campbell Gallery in San Francisco, to form the Campbell-Thiebaud Gallery, San Francisco

1991

Creates *Monotype Variations* at Crown Point Press in San Francisco, which are exhibited at the press's gallery in San Francisco. *Wayne Thiebaud—Three Decades of Still-Lifes* is shown at Associated American Artists gallery in New York. *Wayne Thiebaud* is mounted at the Ahmanson Fine Arts Center at Pepperdine University, Malibu, California, and another show by that title is exhibited at the Carpenter Center for the Visual Arts, Harvard University, Cambridge, Massachusetts

Receives a Governor's Award for the Arts, sponsored by the California Arts Council, in honor of lifetime achievement

1991–1992

Vision and Revision: The Hand-Colored Prints of Wayne Thiebaud is held at the California Palace of the Legion of Honor, San Francisco. The show opens in December 1991 and then travels to the Modern Art Museum of Fort Worth, Texas; the National Museum of American Art, Smithsonian Institution, Washington, DC; and the Norton Museum of Art, West Palm Beach, Florida. Is included in the group show *American Realism and*

Wayne Thiebaud giving a painting demonstration at the University of California, Davis, n.d. Photographer unknown

Figurative Art: 1952–1990 organized at the Miyagi Museum of Art in Sendai, Japan, which travels to the Sogo Museum of Art, Yokohama; the Tokushima Modern Art Museum, Tokushima; the Museum of Modern Art, Shiga; and the Museum of Art, Kōchi

1992

Creates "Celebration Cakes" poster for the University of California's 125th anniversary

UC Davis holds two exhibitions of Thiebaud's work: *Selections from the Collection / Wayne Thiebaud Prints* at the Richard L. Nelson Gallery and *Wayne Thiebaud: Posters from the Collection of Gina Kelsch* at the Walter A. Buehler Alumni Association. *Wayne Thiebaud Still-Lifes* is shown at Graystone Gallery, San Francisco. Work is included in *Hand-Painted Pop: American Art in Transition, 1955–1962*, a group show organized by the Museum of Contemporary Art, Los Angeles, which travels to the Museum of Contemporary Art, Chicago, and the Whitney Museum of American Art, New York

1992–1994

Wayne Thiebaud Prints is organized by the American Federation of Arts at the C. A. Johnson Gallery in Middlebury, Vermont, and travels to the Schneider Museum of Art, Southern Oregon State College (now Southern Oregon University), Ashland, Oregon; the Cheney Cowles Museum (now the Northwest Museum of Arts and Culture), Spokane, Washington; the Heckscher Museum of Art, Huntington, New York; the Colby College Museum of Art, Waterville, Maine; The Butler Institute of American Art, Youngstown, Ohio; the Huntington Museum of Art, Huntington, West Virginia; the Flint Institute of Arts, Flint, Michigan; and the Sheldon Memorial Art Gallery, Lincoln, Nebraska

1993

Wayne Thiebaud: Cityscapes and *Wayne Thiebaud: Figure Drawings* are exhibited at Campbell-Thiebaud Gallery, San Francisco. *Wayne Thiebaud: Still Lifes and Landscapes* is hosted by Associated American Artists gallery, New York. Work is included in *Bay Area Tradition: Robert Bechtle, Christopher Brown, Wayne Thiebaud* at Crown Point Press, San Francisco

Receives an honorary doctor of arts degree from the Art Institute of Southern California, Laguna Beach, and the Grumbacher Gold Medal Award for Painting from the National Academy of Design in New York. Also becomes an honorary member of the California Society of Printmakers

Collaborates with the California Arts Council and the California Department of Motor Vehicles to produce "Coastline," a vanity license plate that raised millions of dollars for California arts organizations and is his most widely distributed work

Begins series of Sacramento–San Joaquin Delta scenes

1994

Allan Stone Gallery exhibits *Wayne Thiebaud and Allan Stone: Celebrating 33 Years Together*. The National Academy of Design, New York, shows *Wayne Thiebaud*. The Wiegand Gallery at the

Gallerist Allan Stone presenting Wayne Thiebaud with an award at The Plaza Hotel, New York, n.d. Photographer unknown

College of Notre Dame in Belmont, California, hosts *Wayne Thiebaud: Figurative Works, 1959–1994*. *Wayne Thiebaud Still Lifes* is held at Crown Point Press, San Francisco, and *Wayne Thiebaud: Prints, 1970–1984* is shown at the A. P. Giannini Gallery at the Bank of America World Headquarters, San Francisco

Receives the National Medal of Arts from President Bill Clinton

1995

Work is included in *Facing Eden: 100 Years of Landscape Art in the Bay Area*, held at the M. H. de Young Memorial Museum, San Francisco. Berggruen Gallery in San Francisco hosts *Wayne Thiebaud: Objects of Desire—Selected Paintings, Works on Paper, and Prints*. Bobby Greenfield Gallery in Santa Monica, California, exhibits *Wayne Thiebaud's Landscapes and Foodscapes*. Crown Point Press, San Francisco, hosts *Wayne Thiebaud and the Gravure Group: Christopher Brown, Tom Marioni, Gay Outlaw, Edward Ruscha*

Is commissioned to create nine lithographs for Arion Press to illustrate a limited edition of Jean Anthelme Brillat-Savarin's *The Physiology of Taste: Or Meditations on Transcendental Gastronomy*, first published in France in 1825. These are exhibited in *Wayne Thiebaud: The Physiology of Taste, 9 New Lithographs*, Jim Kempner Fine Art, New York

Receives the Distinguished Artistic Achievement Award from the California Society of Printmakers in Berkeley, California

1996

Thiebaud Selects Thiebaud: A Forty-Year Survey from Private Collections opens at the Crocker Art Museum. Smaller exhibitions of Thiebaud's works on paper include: *Thiebaud: Original Graphics* at Van Staveren Fine Art, Sacramento, California, and *Wayne Thiebaud* at the Pasadena City College Art Gallery, Pasadena, California. Serves as artist-in-residence, Shatford Library and Boone Sculpture Garden, Pasadena City College.

Receives the Gold Medal for Lifetime Achievement in the Arts Award from the National Arts Club, New York. Also receives Award of Excellence from the National Park Service for an illustration created for a new edition of *Yosemite and the Mariposa Grove: A Preliminary Report, 1865*, written by Frederick Law Olmsted

1997

Wayne Thiebaud is held at Allan Stone Gallery. *Wayne Thiebaud at Crown Point Press* is shown at the Crown Point Press gallery, San Francisco. The Kemper Museum of Contemporary Art in Kansas City, Missouri, exhibits *Wayne Thiebaud: Intimate Prints*. Campbell-Thiebaud Gallery in San Francisco holds *Wayne Thiebaud: Landscapes*, the first exhibition to feature the Sacramento–San Joaquin Delta series. Work is included in *Thirty-Five Years at Crown Point Press: Making Prints, Doing Art*, organized by the National Gallery of Art, Washington, DC, which travels to the California Palace of the Legion of Honor, San Francisco

Receives an honorary doctor of fine arts degree from the Art Institute of Boston (now Lesley University College of Art and Design)

1998

Wayne Thiebaud: Works on Paper from the Family Collections, 1955–1998 opens at the Springfield Art Museum in Springfield, Missouri. The Armory Art Center in West Palm Beach, Florida, exhibits *Singular Visions / Multiple Views*. Work is included in *Artists Contemporary Gallery 40th Anniversary* at the ACG, Sacramento

Receives an honorary doctor of fine arts degree from California State University, Sacramento

1999

Exhibition *Wayne Thiebaud: Simple Delights, Works on Paper, 1963–1979* is held at Campbell-Thiebaud Gallery in Laguna Beach, California. *Wayne Thiebaud: Prints* is shown at Fairbanks Gallery at Oregon State University, Corvallis, Oregon. Arion Press in San Francisco publishes *Invisible Cities* by Italo Calvino with twelve illustrations and an etching by Thiebaud. Work is included in *Innovation and Influence: The Art of Richard Diebenkorn and Wayne Thiebaud* at the Sun Valley Center for the Arts in Ketchum, Idaho, and in *Diebenkorn and Thiebaud: Prints* at Karen McCready Fine Art, New York

2000

Slice of Life: Wayne Thiebaud Paintings and Prints is exhibited at the Crocker Art Museum. *Wayne Thiebaud: A Paintings Retrospective* is held at the California Palace of the Legion of Honor, San Francisco, and subsequently travels to the Modern Art Museum of Fort Worth, Texas; the Phillips Collection, Washington, DC; and the Whitney Museum of American Art, New York. Work is included in *The American Century: Art and Culture, 1900–2000* at the Whitney Museum of American Art. *Wayne Thiebaud: Pastels 1960–2000* is shown at Campbell-Thiebaud Gallery, San Francisco

Receives Medal for Painting from the Skowhegan School of Painting and Sculpture, Madison, Maine

2001

Receives Lifetime Achievement Award for Art from the National Academy of Design, New York

Allan Stone Gallery exhibits *Wayne Thiebaud: Four Decades with the Allan Stone Gallery*. The Corcoran Gallery of Art, Washington, DC, exhibits *The Icing on the Cake: Selected Prints by Wayne Thiebaud. The Private Wayne Thiebaud* is held at Pillsbury and Peters Fine Art in Dallas, Texas

Begins Laguna Beach series featuring bird's-eye views of beachcombers, joyful dogs, sand, and surf

2002

The recently renamed Paul Thiebaud Gallery in San Francisco organizes *Riverscapes*, which travels to the Allan Stone Gallery, and Faggionato Fine Arts, London (2003)

Thiebaud family purchases a condominium in Laguna Beach, California

2003

Frederick R. Weisman Museum of Art at Pepperdine University, Malibu, California, exhibits *Wayne Thiebaud: Works from 1955–2003*, which travels to California State University, Sacramento. The Kemper Museum of Contemporary Art in Kansas City, Missouri, exhibits *Wayne Thiebaud: Fifty Years of Painting. Thiebaud: Works on Paper* is held at The Harrison Gallery, Williamstown, Massachusetts

2004

People, Places, and Things is shown at Paul Thiebaud Gallery, San Francisco. *Wayne Thiebaud: City/Country* is mounted at the Harwood Museum of Art at the University of New Mexico, Taos, New Mexico

Nominated for the Gold Medal for Graphic Art from the American Academy of Arts and Letters, New York. Receives the Distinguished Artist Award for Lifetime Achievement from the College Art Association of America

2005

Wayne Thiebaud Since 1962: A Survey is held at Allan Stone Gallery. *Wayne Thiebaud: Works on Paper 1960–2000* is exhibited at the South Dakota Art Museum, South Dakota State University, Brookings. Berggruen Gallery, San Francisco, shows *Wayne Thiebaud: Prints*

Sacramento Philharmonic Orchestra commissions André Previn to create a musical composition in honor of Thiebaud

2006

Sacramento Philharmonic Orchestra honors Thiebaud with "Night Thoughts," written by André Previn and performed in Sacramento

Work is featured in *The Food Show: The Hungry Eye*, held at the Chelsea Art Museum, New York, and the *Gerald Peters Gallery 20th Anniversary Exhibition*, Dallas, Texas

Allan Stone dies

2007

Receives the Bay Area Treasure Award from the San Francisco Museum of Modern Art

Wayne Thiebaud: Hand Colored Prints and Monotypes is shown at Paul Thiebaud Gallery in San Francisco; *Wayne Thiebaud: Recent Work* is exhibited at Paul Thiebaud Gallery in New York

2007–2010

Laguna Art Museum in Laguna Beach, California, exhibits *Wayne Thiebaud: 70 Years of Painting*, which travels to Springville Museum of Art, Springville, Utah (2008); the Palm Springs Art Museum, Palm Springs, California (2009); Loveland Museum Gallery, Loveland, Colorado (2009); Pasadena Museum of California Art, Pasadena, California (2009–2010); and the San Jose Museum of Art, San Jose, California (2010)

2008

Allan Stone Gallery holds *Wayne Thiebaud: The Figure*. Work is included in *You See: The Early Days of the UC Davis Studio Art Faculty*, an exhibition at the Richard L. Nelson Gallery, UC Davis

2009

Exhibition *Sweets and Treats: Wayne Thiebaud in the Collection of the Norton Simon Museum* is held at the Norton Simon Museum in Pasadena, California. Paul Thiebaud Gallery, San Francisco, mounts *Wayne Thiebaud: Confection Memories*. Faggionato Fine Arts, London, opens *Wayne Thiebaud*

Receives the UC Davis Medal, the highest tribute awarded by the university

2010

Paul LeBaron Thiebaud dies June 19

The Crocker Art Museum presents *Wayne Thiebaud: Homecoming* as one of the opening exhibitions in the Teel Family Pavillion, its new Gwathmey Siegel and Associates Architects building. The traveling exhibition *Wayne Thiebaud: Charcoal Still Lifes 1964–1974* is shown at Lawrence Markey Inc., in San Antonio, and at the Paul Thiebaud Galleries in San Francisco and New York. The Sacramento State University Library Gallery mounts *Wayne Thiebaud: Works on Paper*. Gerald Peters Gallery, Santa Fe, New Mexico, exhibits *Wayne Thiebaud Mountains*. Berggruen Gallery, San Francisco, exhibits *The Road to Here*

Is inducted into the California Hall of Fame, the California Museum, Sacramento

2011

Wayne Thiebaud at Museo Morandi opens at the Museo Morandi in Bologna, Italy. The accompanying exhibition catalogue features an essay by Thiebaud expressing his longtime admiration for Giorgio Morandi's paintings. *Wayne Thiebaud: Mountains* is exhibited at St. Supéry Estate Vineyards and Winery Art Gallery, Rutherford, California

2012

Berggruen Gallery, San Francisco, exhibits *Wayne Thiebaud: Paintings and Works on Paper*. Acquavella Galleries, New York, holds *Wayne Thiebaud: A Retrospective*

2013

Paul Thiebaud Gallery in San Francisco exhibits recent mountain paintings in *Wayne Thiebaud: Memory Mountains*

Receives the California Art Award from the Laguna Art Museum, Laguna Beach, California

The Wayne Thiebaud Foundation, an educational nonprofit, is established

2014

Eight exhibitions of Thiebaud's work take place in New York; San Francisco; Malibu, California; and Laguna Beach, California: Crown Point Press in San Francisco mounts *Wayne Thiebaud: Cityscapes and Landscapes*, an exhibition showcasing a new portfolio of prints. What is now Allan Stone Projects, New York, exhibits *Wayne Thiebaud in Black and White*, *Prints by Wayne Thiebaud* and *Project Room: Wayne Thiebaud Figure Drawings*. Jim Kempner Fine Art in New York exhibits *Cakes and 'Scapes: A Selection of Rare, Unique, and Hand-Colored Prints*. Acquavella Galleries, New York, shows *Wayne Thiebaud*. The Frederick R. Weisman Museum of Art at Pepperdine University, Malibu, mounts *Wayne Thiebaud: Works on Paper, 1948–2004*, which travels to the Napa Valley Museum, Yountville, California. The Laguna Art Museum, Laguna Beach, California, shows *Wayne Thiebaud: American Memories*

Begins drawing and painting a series of clowns

2015

Wayne Thiebaud: Paintings is held at Paul Thiebaud Gallery in San Francisco. *Wayne Thiebaud, By Hand: Works on Paper from 1965–2015* is held at the University Galleries of the University of San Diego. *Wayne Thiebaud: Prints and Works on Paper* is shown at the Sims Reed Gallery, London

Betty Jean Thiebaud dies on December 12

2016

Receives the Lifetime Achievement Award for Innovation from UC Davis

Wayne Thiebaud is held at Allan Stone Projects. Work is shown alongside UC Davis colleagues Robert Arneson and William T. Wiley in *Art of Northern California: Three Views*, San Francisco Museum of Modern Art. University Art Museum, California State University, Long Beach, exhibits *Wayne Thiebaud: Prints in Process*

2017

Wayne Thiebaud: Land Survey opens at Allan Stone Projects, and *Wayne Thiebaud, 1962–2017* is held at the White Cube, London

Completes *Clown Memories* series at Crown Point Press, San Francisco

Participates in *The Artist Project: What Artists See When They Look at Art* at The Metropolitan Museum of Art, New York; his thoughts on Rosa Bonheur's *The Horse Fair* (1852–1855) are featured in a Met publication and a documentary short. "City, River, Mountain: Wayne Thiebaud's California" is published by Margaretta M. Lovell in *Panorama: The Journal of the Association of Historians of American Art*

Receives Gold Medal from the American Academy of Arts and Letters in New York

2018

Wayne Thiebaud: 1958–1968 is held at the newly opened Jan Shrem and Maria Manetti Shrem Museum of Art at UC Davis. *Wayne Thiebaud: Draftsman*, a retrospective of works on paper, is shown at The Morgan Library and Museum, New York. *Wayne Thiebaud*, the artist's first major retrospective in continental Europe, is mounted at the Museum Voorlinden, Wassenaar, the Netherlands

California Landscapes: Richard Diebenkorn / Wayne Thiebaud opens at Acquavella Galleries, New York. *Wayne Thiebaud: Monotypes* is shown at Paul Thiebaud Gallery, San Francisco

2018–2019

Thiebaud curates *Artist's Choice*, an exhibition at the San Francisco Museum of Modern Art (SFMOMA) in which he selects objects for display from the museum's permanent collection and works with museum staff on the exhibition design. This exhibition accompanies *Wayne Thiebaud: Paintings and Drawings*, a smaller show featuring works by Thiebaud from SFMOMA's permanent collection, including recent gifts to the museum from the Thiebaud family

2019

Wayne Thiebaud Mountains: 1965–2019 is exhibited at Acquavella Galleries, New York. *Works by Wayne Thiebaud* held at the John Natsoulas Center for the Arts in Davis, California, in honor of Thiebaud's 99th birthday

2020

Paul Thiebaud Gallery in San Francisco opens *Clowns*, the first exhibition of Thiebaud's recent clown-themed series

Wayne Thiebaud 100: Paintings, Prints, and Drawings (October 2020–January 2021) is held at the Crocker Art Museum in celebration of Thiebaud's 100th birthday. The exhibition subsequently travels to Toledo Museum of Art, Toledo, Ohio; Dixon Gallery and Gardens, Memphis, Tennessee; McNay Art Museum, San Antonio; and Brandywine Conservancy and Museum of Art, Chadds Ford, Pennsylvania

SELECTED PUBLICATIONS

1965

Figures: Thiebaud. Introduction by Gerald M. Ackerman. Artist statement by Wayne Thiebaud. Stanford, CA: Stanford University Press, 1965.

1967

Wayne Thiebaud. New York: Allan Stone Gallery, 1967.

1968

Coplans, John. *Wayne Thiebaud*. Pasadena, CA: Pasadena Art Museum, 1968.

Taylor, John Lloyd. *Thiebaud*. Milwaukee, WI: Milwaukee Art Center, 1968.

1970

Recent Works by Wayne Thiebaud. Introduction by John A. Mahey. Sacramento, CA: E. B. Crocker Art Gallery, 1970.

1971

Wayne Thiebaud Graphics: 1964–1971. New York: Parasol Press, 1971.

1972

Cooper, Gene. *Wayne Thiebaud: Survey of Paintings 1950–1972*. Long Beach, CA: School of Fine Art, California State University, 1972.

1976

Cooper, Gene. *Wayne Thiebaud: Survey 1947–1976*. Foreword by Ronald D. Hickman. Preface by Donald J. Brewer. Phoenix: Phoenix Art Museum, 1976.

1980

Wayne Thiebaud: Paintings, Pastels, Drawings and Prints. Introduction by Wayne Thiebaud. San Francisco: John Berggruen Gallery, San Francisco, 1980.

1981

Beal, Graham W. J. *Wayne Thiebaud: Paintings*. Minneapolis: Walker Art Center, 1981.

1982

Wayne Thiebaud. Introduction by Gene Cooper. Santa Cruz, CA: Art Museum of Santa Cruz County, 1982.

1983

Clisby, Roger D. *Wayne Thiebaud: Landscapes and City Views*. Sacramento, CA: Crocker Art Museum, 1983.

Wayne Thiebaud: Paintings, Drawings, Graphics 1961–1983. Introduction by David Alan Robertson. Carlisle, PA: Dickinson College, 1983.

1985

Tsujimoto, Karen. *Wayne Thiebaud*. Foreword by Henry T. Hopkins. Chronology by Donna Graves. Exhibition History by Donna Graves and Kathleen Butler. Bibliography by Eugenie Candau. San Francisco and Seattle: San Francisco Museum of Modern Art and University of Washington Press, 1985.

1987

Berkson, Bill. *Wayne Thiebaud Works on Paper: From the Collection of the Artist*, Chicago: Arts Club of Chicago, 1987.

Glenn, Constance and Jack Glenn, ed. *Wayne Thiebaud: Private Drawings, The Artist's Sketchbook*. New York: Harry N. Abrams, 1987.

1990

Harlow, Ann. *Thiebaud at Seventy*. Moraga, CA: Saint Mary's College, 1990.

Shone, Richard. *Wayne Thiebaud: Prints and Hand-Coloured Etchings*. London: Karsten Schubert, 1990.

1993

Bahet, Kathleen. *Wayne Thiebaud: Still Lifes & Landscapes*. New York: Associated American Artists, New York, 1993.

Dalkey, Victoria. *Wayne Thiebaud: Figure Drawings*. San Francisco: Campbell-Thiebaud Gallery, 1993.

Wayne Thiebaud: Cityscapes. Interview with Wayne Thiebaud by Richard Wollheim. San Francisco: Campbell-Thiebaud Gallery, 1993.

1994

Wayne Thiebaud at Allan Stone Gallery: Celebrating 33 Years Together. Introduction by Allan Stone. New York: Allan Stone Gallery, 1994.

Wayne Thiebaud Figurative Works 1959–1994. Introduction by Charles Strong. Interview with Wayne Thiebaud by Bill Berkson. South Bend, IN: Wiegand Gallery, College of Notre Dame, 1994.

1996

McGough, Stephen C. *Thiebaud Selects Thiebaud: A Forty-Year Survey from Private Collections*. Sacramento, CA: Crocker Art Museum, 1996.

1997

Dalkey, Victoria. *Wayne Thiebaud: Landscapes*. Foreword by Paul LeBaron Thiebaud. San Francisco: Campbell-Thiebaud Gallery, 1997.

2000

Nash, Steven A., and Adam Gopnik. *Wayne Thiebaud: A Paintings Retrospective*. San Francisco: Fine Arts Museums of San Francisco, 2000.

Wayne Thiebaud: Pastels 1960–2000. Introduction by Paul LeBaron Thiebaud. San Francisco: Campbell-Thiebaud Gallery, 2000.

2002

Wayne Thiebaud: Riverscapes. Introduction by Paul LeBaron Thiebaud, Allan Stone, and Gerard Faggionato. San Francisco: Paul Thiebaud Gallery, 2002.

2003

Wayne Thiebaud: Fifty Years of Painting. Foreword by Dana Self. Interview with Wayne Thiebaud by Rachael Blackburn. Kansas City, MO: Kemper Museum of Contemporary Art, 2003.

Zakian, Michael, and Elaine O'Brien. *Wayne Thiebaud: Works from 1955 to 2003*. Malibu, CA, and Sacramento, CA: Frederick R. Weisman Museum of Art, Pepperdine University and University Library Gallery, California State University, Sacramento, 2003.

2004

Wayne Thiebaud: City/Country. Introduction by Charles M. Lovell. Interview with Wayne Thiebaud by Charles Strong. Taos, NM: Harwood Museum of Art, University of New Mexico, 2004.

2005

Kuspit, Donald. *Wayne Thiebaud: Paintings*. London: Faggionato Fine Art, 2005.

2007

Cooper, Gene. *Thiebaud: Seventy Years of Painting*. Laguna Beach, CA: Laguna Art Museum, 2007.

You See: The Early Years of the UC Davis Studio Art Faculty. Davis, CA: Richard L. Nelson Gallery, University of California, Davis, 2007.

2008

Tsujimoto, Karen. *Wayne Thiebaud: The Figure*. New York, Allan Stone Gallery, 2008.

2009

Nash, Steven A., and Gene Cooper. *Wayne Thiebaud: 70 Years of Painting*. Palm Springs, CA: Palm Springs Art Museum, 2009.

2010

Anfam, David. *Wayne Thiebaud*. London and New York: Faggionato Fine Art and Paul Thiebaud Gallery, 2010.

Berkson, Bill. *Wayne Thiebaud: Charcoal Still Lifes 1964–1974*. San Antonio, TX, and San Francisco: Lawrence Markey Inc. and Paul Thiebaud Gallery, 2010.

Hughes, Robert. *Wayne Thiebaud: Mountains*. Introduction by Gerald Peters. Santa Fe, NM: Gerald Peters Gallery, 2010.

2011

Masi, Alessia. *Wayne Thiebaud at Museo Morandi*. Mantua, Italy: Corraini Edizioni, 2011.

2012

Wilmerding, John, and Pepe Karmel. *Wayne Thiebaud*. Foreword by William R. Acquavella. New York: Acquavella Galleries, 2012.

2014

Aschheim, Eve, and Chris Daubert. *Episodes with Wayne Thiebaud: Four Interviews 2009–2011*. New York: Black Square Editions, 2014.

Ratcliff, Carter. *Wayne Thiebaud: In Black and White*. New York: Allan Stone Projects, 2014.

Reynolds, Jock. *Wayne Thiebaud*. New York: Acquavella Galleries, 2014.

Zakian, Michael. *Wayne Thiebaud: Works on Paper 1948–2004*. Malibu, CA: Frederick R. Weisman Museum of Art, Pepperdine University, 2014.

2015

Baker, Kenneth, Nicolas Fox Weber, Karen Wilkin, and John Yau. *Wayne Thiebaud*. New York: Rizzoli, 2015.

2017

Anfam, David. *Wayne Thiebaud 1962 to 2017*. London: White Cube, 2017.

2018

Yau, John, and Richard Diebenkorn. Conversations with Wayne Thiebaud by Philippe de Montebello and Richard Wollheim. *California Landscapes: Richard Diebenkorn, Wayne Thiebaud*. New York: Acquavella Galleries, 2018.

Dervaux, Isabelle. *Wayne Thiebaud, Draftsman*. Foreword by Colin B. Bailey. New York: Morgan Library and Museum in association with Thames and Hudson, 2018.

Swarts, Suzanne, Wayne Thiebaud, Steven Aalders, Laura Cumming, and Rudi Fuchs. *Wayne Thiebaud*. Wassenaar, the Netherlands: Museum Voorlinden, 2018.

Teagle, Rachel, Margaretta Lovell, and Alexander Nemerov. Foreword by Ralph J. Hexter. Plate entries by Francesca Wilmott. Chronology by Arielle Hardy. *Wayne Thiebaud: 1958–1968*. Davis, CA: Jan Shrem and Maria Manetti Shrem Museum of Art, University of California, Davis, in association with The University of California Press, 2018.

2019

Thiebaud, Wayne, Janet Bishop, Derrick R. Cartwright, Kathan Brown, Fred Dalkey, Victoria Dalkey, Steve Nash, Scott A. Shields, Clay Vorhes, Malcolm Warner, and Michael Zakian. *Thiebaud Delicious Metropolis: The Desserts and Urban Scenes of Wayne Thiebaud*. San Francisco: Chronicle Books, 2019.

Lovell, Margaretta M., and Michael M. Thomas. *Wayne Thiebaud Mountains: 1965–2019*. New York: Acquavella Galleries, 2019.

INDEX

Page numbers in italics refer to illustrations. Unless otherwise noted, all works are by Wayne Thiebaud.

100